CW00548350

HAPPINESS OUTSIDE THE STATE

HAPPINESS OUTSIDE THE STATE

Judaism, Christianity, Islam
Three Ways to God

IGNAZ MAYBAUM

ORIEL PRESS
STOCKSFIELD

HENLEY   BOSTON   LONDON

First published in 1980
by Oriel Press Ltd. (Routledge & Kegan Paul Ltd.)
Branch End, Stocksfield,
Northumberland, NE43 7NA

Printed and bound in Great Britain
by Knight and Forster Ltd., Leeds

ISBN 0 85362 183 7

TO
MY GRANDCHILDREN
MIRIAM, SIMON, NAOMI, REBECCA
AND
NINA AND GABY

CONTENTS

PREFACE

The Middle East is a term created by the modern historian. Our forefathers spoke of the Holy Land. The Holy Land lies surrounded by nations whose history goes back to Semitic antiquity.

When Napoleon entered Egypt, he brought western ideas to the orient. The turmoil of the French Revolution awakened the orient. To the Jewish people the French Revolution came in the nineteenth century; with the slogan 'Reform', Jews began to scrutinise their Orthodox form of life and learnt to reject much of what had been meticulously preserved for centuries. When Jews came to Palestine in the late nineteenth and early twentieth century, Arabs marvelled at these westernised Jews. Did they come in search of the Holy Land? The Holy Land became a domain of westernised life.

There are three ways in which a man belonging to monotheistic civilization can experience holiness. First there is terrestrial holiness, which is bound to a place on the map. This holiness is connected with a country or a city. To many people, not only to the Muslim, terrestrial holiness is very dear. Millions who have died willingly for the nation state were motivated by terrestrial holiness. One need not be a Muslim to have one's 'Mecca'. Jerusalem, Rome, Wittenberg, Weimar are places of terrestrial holiness.

Secondly, there is spiritual holiness. Unconsummated love is spiritual love. It makes the Christian. He experiences holiness as soaring high above life and yet real. The Christian spiritualises events which happened, bringing a new era into history. These spiritual events are the hard facts which the Christian recaptures on his pilgrimage. Christian holiness is spiritual holiness.

The Jewish concept of holiness is explained by the commandment 'You shall be holy, because I, the Lord your God, am holy' (Leviticus 19, 2). Holiness, in this case, is demanded from all men and is a universally understandable experience.

I often speak of monotheistic civilization and prefer this term to the terms Judaism, Christianity or Islam. With the term monotheistic civilization I hold the view that all three monotheistic forms of expressing holiness have equal capacity to contribute to the one world religion, which has its birthplace in the Middle East. Today the Middle East is again becoming, in all the travail which we witness with deep concern, the birthplace of the revival of monotheism, uniting Jew, Christian and Muslim in their search for terrestrial holiness, spiritual holiness and that holiness which is human and universal. This unity can be the very aim to which Jew, Christian and Muslim aspire. The whole world looks to the Middle East. I speak of a new era in the Middle East.

My book consists of papers which I have read to students of the Leo Baeck College (for the Training of Progressive Ministers). As a teacher I have followed the pedagogical rule of always returning to my main subject. Therefore there will be some repetitions in the book. They are needed for the understanding of my theme. I continue in this book with ideas which I have outlined in my book *Trialogue Between Jew, Christian and Muslim* (The Littman Library of Jewish Civilization, Routledge & Kegan Paul, London, 1973). When I refer in my text to this book I abbreviate the title to *Trialogue*. When I quote, as I often do, Franz Rosenzweig's *Star of Redemption* (The Littman Library of Jewish Civilization, Routledge & Kegan Paul, London, 1971) I speak of the '*Star*'. The work of Martin Buber is well known in England and America, but the theological work of Franz Rosenzweig is only beginning to have its impact on the English-speaking world.

Part I of the Summary is an excerpt of a lecture given under the auspices of the *Standing Conference of Jews, Christians and Muslims in Europe (British Branch)*.

Ignaz Maybaum

This book was completed by the end of 1975. The author was not able to submit it to the publishers himself, as he died in March 1976. On his behalf I would like to thank all those who have made the publication of the book possible through creation of the Ignaz Maybaum Memorial Fund, by contributing to and working for it. My thanks go to the Chairman of the Edgware and District Reform Synagogue, to the Chairman of Leo Baeck College, to all the other Synagogues within the Reform Synagogues of Great Britain and to the friends of my late husband outside these Synagogues in this country and overseas.

I would also like to express my deepfelt gratitude—as my husband would have done—to his former pupil and later colleague Rabbi Dr. N. R. M. de Lange, Lecturer in Rabbinics in the University of Cambridge, for the devotion with which he read the manuscript and for the valuable suggestions he made while reading it.

I am also indebted to him for the continuing help and advice he has given me before and during the publication of this book.

Frances Maybaum
Edgware, January 1979

FOREWORD

This book has lost nothing of its freshness and relevance in the four years between completion and publication. On the contrary, in the light of recent displays of "justice" in newly created Islamic republics, the author's analysis of Islam as "monotheism without prophecy" becomes especially significant and poignant.

Ignaz Maybaum's primary concern, however, was not Islam as such, and definitely not its current political manifestations, but the influence of Islamic thought on Judaism. By identifying Orthodoxy's preoccupation with law as "Islamised Judaism" and as "Judaism without prophecy", he has placed it in sharp contrast to the prophetic Judaism of the liberal camp.

The repudiation of Jewish legalism should not be misunderstood as a rejection of tradition and observance. The record of Maybaum's ministry in Germany and in Britain testifies to that, as did his own home life. The theological basis for his affirmation of tradition, despite the rejection of legalism, is reflected in his declaration that "the house is and remains the abode of the Jew", the place where "the holy family of the secular age dwells." Whereas his theology makes Maybaum one of the most significant thinkers of our generation, it is his simultaneous critique of soulless legalism and acceptance of such observance which makes for holiness that establishes him as the exponent *par excellence* of British Reform.

It is the stress on the holiness of house and family that prompted Maybaum to express reservations about the State, any State including the Jewish State, since it so easily threatens the bourgeois life. For Maybaum reality is to be sought in the close circle of the family, in the daily pursuits of fathers, mothers and children which make for holiness and enable each one to experience God. Happiness is not to be attained on the arena of history but in the daily quest for sanctity. That is the message of this book.

To see Maybaum as an opponent of Zionism would be to misunderstand him radically, especially in the light of his courageous espousal of the Zionist cause in pre-war Germany, when such an act on the part of a liberal rabbi was almost unheard of. But his concern for domestic holiness in juxtaposition to political secularism, his repudiation of blind obedience to man-made law (Halacha) in place of humble commitment to God's teaching (Torah) made him critical of the Jewish State. Instead he saw the justification of Jewish existence in every place where Jews were allowed to live as free men. That includes, of course, also Israel. He refused to negate the Diaspora. On the contrary, he recognised it as a vehicle for prophetic Judaism and as such a blue-print for human existence as a whole. The Biblical injunction, "You shall be holy, for I the Lord your God am holy", was the basis for his understanding of historic as well as contemporary Judaism.

Maybaum's conception of Judaism made him critical not only of Islam and of secular politics but also of Christianity, which he had identified in earlier writings as one of the sources of the Holocaust and as a force that makes for secularisation. But it is not an obscurantist isolationism that he preaches; his aim is dialogue. Like other modern Jewish theologians he seeks a framework for a dialogue with Christianity, but, unlike most of them, he adds another dimension by bringing in Islam. In Maybaum's writings the dialogue is expanded into a trialogue, for he insists that only thus will we be able to understand ourselves as Jews as well as understand the culture in the midst of which we live.

As he himself pointed out in the Preface, this book continues the line of his *Trialogue between Jew, Christian and Muslim*. Many of the ideas could also be traced to earlier works and one of our future tasks must be to publish a systematic edition of a representative selection of his writings in which the development of each theme could be clearly shown and the relationship to other themes properly illustrated. In this way the range and depth of Maybaum's teachings could be made easily accessible to future generations.

That those who will come after us will wish to learn from him is beyond doubt. In the same way as his lectures at the Leo Baeck College, which formed the basis of five or six of his books, came to shape this generation of rabbis, so will his writings come to influence those who will succeed us. It is, therefore, significant that his posthumously published book should be dedicated to his grand-children, for it points to a future which only they will fully understand and appreciate. We who read the book now are grateful to be stirred by the prophetic message it contains. By learning from it and responding to it critically, we will pay its author the best memorial tribute he could have wished for himself.

Dow Marmur

BIBLIOGRAPHY

Works by *IGNAZ MAYBAUM (1897-1976)*
Books

Parteibefreites Judentum: Lehrende Führung und priesterliche Gemeinschaft.
Philo Verlag, Berlin 1935.

Neue Jugend und alter Glaube: Der Chaluz und der Baal-habajit in der Verantwortung vor der Lehre.
Philo Verlag, Berlin 1936.

Man and Catastrophe.
Allenson & Co. Ltd, London 1941

Synagogue and Society: Jewish-Christian Collaboration in the Defence of Western Civilisation.
James Clarke & Co. Ltd, London 1943.

The Jewish Home.
James Clarke & Co. Ltd, London 1945.

The Jewish Mission.
James Clarke & Co. Ltd, London 1949.

Jewish Existence.
Vallentine, Mitchell, London 1960.

The Faith of the Jewish Diaspora.
Vision Press Ltd, London 1962.

The Face of God after Auschwitz
Polak & Van Gennep Ltd, Amsterdam 1965.

Creation and Guilt: A Theological Assessment of Freud's Father-Son Conflict.
Vallentine, Mitchell, London 1969.

Trialogue between Jew, Christian and Muslim
Routledge & Kegan Paul, London 1973.

HAPPINESS OUTSIDE THE STATE

I

Liturgical Controversy

Jew, Christian and Muslim at Prayer

SINCE when do we sing in synagogue? Jewish research, if such research exists at all, does not answer this question. One thing is certain: the singing worshipper was not to be found in the prayer gathering of the Pharisees of old.

Defining the difference between Judaism and Christianity, both Franz Rosenzweig and Leo Baeck state that in faith and worship the Christian rises to the sphere called spiritual. The Jew does not need the services of the spiritual to meet God. One need not be a trained musicologist to find out how the element of the spiritual is expressed musically. The soprano voices, soaring out jubilantly, create a spiritual atmosphere. Such an atmosphere is there in a Christian church. Does it mean that a spiritual atmosphere must be absent in a synagogue? We must deal carefully with this question and must not rush to the conclusion of some Jews to whom the female soprano voices in a choir seem somehow un-Jewish. Spirituality is a Christian experience but Christianity is an offspring of Judaism. No outright condemnation of the spiritual elements, if they are to be found in a synagogue service, can be justified by the Jew. But it is advisable to avoid a predominance of the spiritual atmosphere.

The exuberant singing, especially of the soprano voices, creates the numinous atmosphere in church and synagogue alike. But there is something else at the disposal of the worshipper besides devout singing: the words of the prayer book, spoken by the Jewish worshipper. The Jewish worshipper is a 'book-reading worshipper', as I called him in my *Trialogue between Jew, Christian and Muslim* (p. 27). The word spoken by man, by the praying worshipper, can be embellished by spiritu-

1

ality, by poetry and music, but remains a word spoken in prose. A homiletics teacher at Leo Baeck College warned the students not to read the prayers like a piece of poetry. The numinous atmosphere in a synagogue is created by the insistence of the worshipper not to enter the aesthetic realm. With the medium of the spoken word alone the worshipper is never a creator but stands, praying, as a creature before God. Bach's music, performed in a church, is both sublime and religious and is also a piece of art. Art has a limited place in a mosque and none in a synagogue. The commandment of the decalogue not to make an image of anything is strictly observed. Worshipping through the medium of the spoken word makes the prayer Jewish prayer: prayer is not aesthetic uplift. Aesthetic uplift is the wonderful gift which art bestows on man. But prayer can and indeed must be something other than aesthetic uplift. Prayer in church invokes the help of the uplift of art. Between Jewish prayer with the exclusive help of the spoken word and Christian prayer using the assistance of art there is a difference of which we must remain aware. The spoken word as the only constituent of the numinous atmosphere in a synagogue makes Rosenzweig say: 'Prose is our poetry'.

Theologians have so far not discovered that two different kinds of divine service exist within the Jewish community itself. Most Jews need, as they say jokingly, two Synagogues: one in which they worship, and one in which 'they would not be seen dead'. These Jewish fighters for the true Synagogue do not even have names at their disposal when they discuss the two forms of Jewish worship. The Yiddish word *davnen* has the same root as the Latin word *divinus*. *Davnen* is the praying of worshippers who radically exclude the other form of service, which I propose to call hymnal service. These two services must not be understood as in the one case Orthodox, in the other Progressive. They concern liturgical, not doctrinal distinctions. A cantor, overstressing the performance of his musical contribution, can transform an Orthodox Synagogue into a place of hymnal service. The choir of a Progressive Synagogue, on the other hand, which allows the participation of the worshippers, can acquire the same numinous density as a service

2

characterised by the devotion of *davening*.

The choice between the two services must not be made on aesthetic grounds. Any choice on these grounds is a wrong one. There are social reasons which force Jews to opt for a particular kind of service. When, with the Emancipation, great Jewish communities were established in western capitals, the hymnal service became frequent in the synagogue. But communities in the provinces with a small number of congregants, without a musically trained cantor and choir, loved and upheld the form of prayer which is denoted by the medieval word *davnen*. In an American-Yiddish novel the phrase *'Daven* with us' is translated as *'Read* with us'.

Finally, the term *davnen*, although it is a Yiddish word, shows the proximity of synagogue and mosque. There is no music and no singing in a mosque. The praying Muslim, it can be said, *davens*, as does the Jew in the Synagogue. Both Jew and Muslim are concerned in their prayer with the spoken words and do without the spirituality of the hymnal service. The Orthodox Jew, accompanying the words of his prayer with movements of his body, and the Muslim, acting in the same way in his worship, show how near the Orthodox Jew and the Muslim stand to each other. Other points which illustrate this nearness will be noted in the following chapters.

Abraham Geiger and Samson Raphael Hirsch

The controversy between the two nineteenth-century rabbis Abraham Geiger* and Samson Raphael Hirsch is about Isaiah 40-53. This text from the book of Isaiah refers to the so-called Jewish Mission. We are dealing with a confrontation between Jewish messianism and Jewish pietism. It clarifies the situation of modern Jewry if we recognise the term 'Jewish Orthodoxy' as a misnomer in the case of S.R. Hirsch. It is Jewish pietism, not Jewish Orthodoxy, with which we are really dealing. As any scholar of comparative religion will state, a new chapter of

*Ludwig Geiger, *Abraham Geiger, Leben und Lebenswerk*, Georg Reimer, Berlin, 1910; Paul Volz, *Jesaia II* (Kommentar zum Alten Testament, Band IX) Leipzig, 1932; Harry M. Orlinsky, *Studies of the Second Part of the Book of Isaiah*, E. J. Brill, Leiden, 1967.

history does not start as Orthodoxy. S. R. Hirsch, usually described as an Orthodox rabbi, leads, just like Geiger, into the new chapter of German-Jewish renaissance. Both are products of the liberal nineteenth century, Geiger expressing his messianism with the help of liberal ideology and Hirsch using the same means to make his pietism articulate.

Samson Raphael Hirsch, the rabbi of a congregation in Frankfurt on Main, was the mouthpiece of the *Landjuden* (country Jews) who had left the little villages around Frankfurt and had settled in the town. They remained *Landjuden* even as citizens of Frankfurt. They had become affluent but did not become intellectuals. In his sermons S. R. Hirsch spoke about Judaism in a way which warmed the hearts of his flock but made all the new Jewish intelligentsia who demanded a scholarly approach to Judaism despair. For them Geiger was the preacher. The tension between the intellectual interpretation of Judaism and romantic influence was retained by German Jewry throughout its whole history.

Samson Raphael Hirsch is seen as an Orthodox rabbi. But he is under an influence which is no longer that of the medieval code of the *Shulhan Arukh*. This code distinguished between Jew and gentile. Hirsch distinguished between Jew and Jew. Hirsch represented the Jew who was a Jew through his rooted-ness in the worshipping congregation and who was not messian-ically motivated. Pietism, not messianism, was the Judaism which Hirsch disseminated in Frankfurt. Geiger's Judaism was messianism.

In his messianism Geiger insisted on what Zionists later called 'the solution of the Jewish question'. At the time when Moses Montefiore moved heaven and earth to bring help to his brethren in the Orient, Geiger wrote to Josef Derenbourg of the Alliance Israélite Universelle (22nd November 1840): 'That Jews in Prussia should be entitled to enter the liberal pro-fessions (literally: to become chemists and lawyers) seems to me more important than the rescue of all the Jews in Africa and Asia, which, as a man, I have at heart'.

Geiger was a kind-hearted man. As a man he had deep sympathy for the Jews in Damascus. But as a politician, he felt,

he must not be influenced by it. He wanted a solution of the
Jewish question, the end of the *galut*. Once the solution of the
Jewish question was achieved in Germany and in the other
countries of western civilization, 'the still uneducated nations
must follow suit' (letter to Derenbourg of 5th August 1840).
Like the Zionists fifty years later, he did not believe in philan-
thropy. He wanted a political solution. Therefore, as a politician, he could do nothing for the Jews of Damascus.

The messianically motivated Abraham Geiger wanted to see
the rabbis in a new role. He 'demythologized' the rabbis. Geiger
saw the Jews who were working in the professions in the role of
rabbis. The rabbi must be an equal of the modern Jews whom
he loved to see rise to the professions. Jews as lawyers, teachers,
especially university teachers, should be the mentors of the
Jewish people. In nineteenth-century Germany this messianic
dream of Geiger did not remain a dream. It became a reality.
Many were the happy ones who left the *Yeshiva* and went to
study at a western university. The consequence was a social
structure based on a great number of professionals. With the
gentiles it was different. The intellectuals, an élite, were out-
numbered by a majority of peasants and workers. The Zionists
saw this abnormal social structure as a danger to the Jewish
people and aimed at an economic normalisation. Geiger, on the
other hand, hailed the great number of Jewish intellectuals as a
fulfilment for which he had craved in in his messianic dream.
'Your children shall all be instructed by the Lord, and your
sons shall enjoy great prosperity' (Isaiah 54, 13). Rosenzweig,
however, put this verse at the head of his pamphlet *The Buil-
ders*, in which he pleaded for changing the belief in culture and
intellectualism into the pursuit of true Jewish learning. Geiger's
utopian dream came true and a Jewish people came into existence which utilised its great intellectual gifts and differed from
the gentiles with their 'normal' economic structure. This is the
simple explanation of the intellectual characteristics of the Jewish people, and Lord Snow's theory of the special genes in the
body of the Jew is nonsense. Isaiah's words 'He made my
tongue his sharp sword' (49, 2) see the Jew as 'a light to the
nations' and a teacher to them. The proper leader of men is not a

king, not a person in possession of power, but a teacher.

Hirsch rejected Geiger's new understanding of the rabbi. He did not desire to see his flock as intellectuals and professionals having the authority of learned men. He wanted them in meek piety. He also rejected the very phrase 'Jewish Mission' and replaced it with the term 'Jewish Vocation'. Hirsch demanded pietism and always saw messianism as dangerous Sabbatian messianism. Pietism creates cohesive togetherness; messianism, Hirsch argued, dissolves the Jewish people into independent individuals. Here Hirsch saw rightly but judged wrongly what he saw.

Pietism is not identical with Orthodoxy. Hirsch's deep pietism did not make him an Orthodox rabbi. Hirsch was, just like Geiger, a nineteenth-century rabbi, a western Jew far removed from the world of the medieval codes. Those who fail to see the common ground on which both Abraham Geiger and S. R. Hirsch stand will derive a wholesome lesson from the strong criticism which Hirsch encountered in his rabbinic post in Nicolsburg (Moravia) in the years 1847-51. The defenders of the old times looked on Hirsch, whom a later generation celebrated as the founder of Orthodoxy, as a Reformer. In his synagogue service everything was regulated in the minutest detail. Was that not reform? And what strange innovation was introduced at the solemnisation of marriages? Hirsch stopped the custom of celebrating weddings taking place in the open air; he performed the ceremony in the synagogue and gave an address to the bridal couple. Was this not reform? It was also a strange and new thing that Hirsch came to synagogue on Sabbath in a frock coat and a white tie. Was this the way a *Landrabbiner* should appear in public? They all still remembered Rabbi Mordecai Benet, a predecessor of Hirsch in Nicolsburg, who had walked through the streets in a long silk kaftan and a tall fur hat.

One cannot say that the critics who branded S. R. Hirsch as a Reform rabbi dwelt only on the surface of things. They were well aware of a major change in religious life itself. Both Abraham Geiger and S. R. Hirsch put the Bible, put the word of Prophetic Judaism, into the centre of their message.

6

The critics of S. R. Hirsch in Nicolsburg saw how he pro-
ceeded as a teacher in the *Beth-Hamidrash*. He lectured about
the Psalms. What head of a *Beth-Hamidrash* before Hirsch had
troubled to introduce the Psalms into the work of his adult
students? They had learned them as children. The *tehillim*
(Psalms) were said in the form of a litany by pious men and
women on all occasions. Hence the expression *tillim sogen*, the
saying of the Psalms. They were 'said' as prayers were said, not
'learnt'. Now S. R. Hirsch, the new rabbi, treated the Psalms as
seriously as if they were a rabbinical code or the Talmud. The
Dayanim sighed: 'in our days we *learned* Gemara (Talmud) and
said tehillim; now they *learn* tehillim and *say* the Gemara'. They
saw clearly that a change had taken place.

Hirsch's pietism eventually became an irrationalism hostile
to reason and to an intelligent interpretation of biblical texts.
Any western Jew should find what Hirsch wrote in his book
Horeb — The Duties of Israel unacceptable. There he says: 'A
Jew is a true Jew, even if he never understood the meaning of a
single commandment of the *Torah*.' With this statement Hirsch
steps out of the world of the prophets and classical rabbis. This
statement may fit into the world of Islam but even in Islam there
are scholars who would oppose it.

But a defence of Hirsch is possible. He was not a scholar who
could put his views in systematic order. He was a passionate
preacher. In the following lines he contradicted his own Jewish
pietism. In the preacher's passion he exclaimed: '. . . it would
be the best cure to close — provisionally — all synagogues for a
hundred years. Do not tremble at the thought of it, Jewish
heart. What would happen? Jews and Jewesses without
synagogues desiring to remain such would be forced to concen-
trate on a Jewish life and a Jewish home. The Jewish officials
connected with the synagogue would have to look for the only
opportunity now open to them to teach young and old how to
live a Jewish life and how to build a Jewish home. All
synagogues closed by Jewish hands would constitute the
strongest protest against the abandonment of the Torah in
home and life . . .' We need a place of assembly where the
community prays together and hears the Reading of the Law.

This assembly S. R. Hirsch called *Beth-Haknesset,* House of Assembly, and he does not wish to identify it with what his contemporaries called the synagogue.

What a man, this rabbi of Frankfurt on Main! Like a prophet of old he attacked the belief that synagogues in themselves are sufficient. Even today his attacks on the synagogues stagger the reader.

Both Hirsch and Geiger were irritated by the passages in the prayer book which refer to a return to Zion. About Isaiah 2, 3, 'For out of Zion shall go forth the Law, and the word of the Lord from Jerusalem', Geiger says : 'For us it may mean "for out of Zion came forth the Law" instead of 'shall go forth' (*Jüdische Zeitschrift,* Vol. 6, p.8). 'That', remarked Schechter, 'is an amusingly ungrammatical interpretation.' Rab Huna, who died in 296 C.E., said: 'We, living in Babylon, regard ourselves as equal to those living in the Land of Israel' (*Gittin* 6a). With texts like the statement of Rab Huna both Hirsch and Geiger soothed the conscience of the German Jews who were hesitant to call a Germany where they had citizen rights *galut.*

The correspondence between Geiger and Hirsch is revealing. Geiger, who affirmed messianism, became more and more silent concerning the concept of a Jewish Mission. His reason was the determined rejection of the concept of vicarious suffering which he rightly regarded as a Christian dogma. Hirsch, on the other hand, who was reluctant to accept the concept of a Jewish Mission, agreed with the historian Graetz's view of Jewish history as martyrology. He was romantically attached to the figure of the 'suffering' servant. Geiger rejected Hirsch and Graetz with the passionate statement that 'we have suffered enough', as the Zionists formulated it later.

The dogma of vicarious suffering is contradicted by Ezekiel's teaching of individual responsibility: 'It is the soul that sins, and no other, that shall die; a son shall not share a father's guilt, nor a father his son's. The righteous man shall reap the fruit of his own righteousness, and the wicked man the fruit of his own wickedness' (18, 20). Atonement exists. There is no message bringing more happiness to man. But it is from God that we receive these good tidings.

Geiger was irritated by the word servant. Antisemitic scholars see Judaism as a pariah religion. Does not the word *eved* (servant) prove them right? Yet today's modern commentaries point in a different direction. The Great King of Babylon is surrounded by his court of officials and one of them, the most important of them, is the *eved*, the servant. *Eved,* therefore, does not mean slave, but the Chief Minister who is near to the Babylonian Great King and sees that his commands are fulfilled. So far the commentary of Paul Volz. The commentary of Orlinsky points to the agricultural society in which *eved* stands simply for worker. But Geiger, with the Protestant commentaries available in his time, kept away from an interpretation which did not allow him to see the Servant of God, a biblical prophet, in the bright light of freedom. Man is free and not a slave. Geiger therefore deprived himself of the use which the figure of the Servant of God offered him.

Are we today better off than Geiger and Hirsch who were so reluctant to open their hearts to the figure of the Servant of God as described by the commentaries of their time? Have we today better commentaries? Each generation must read the biblical texts and themselves create the commentary which provides the key to right understanding. Geiger saw clearly that his generation still lacked a Jewish commentary to the passages about the Servant of God. Now modern biblical exegesis has emancipated itself from Christian dogma.

To the nineteenth-century Christian commentators the Servant of God was only another expression for the 'Lamb of God'. Geiger, although unable to contradict them on the basis of his own researches, did well to ignore their explanation. His feeling that they were wrong, the feeling of the Jew with all the rabbinical commentaries guiding him, was absolutely right. This can be proved today, with the more recent commentaries.

No quotation from the Book of Isaiah was repeated as often by nineteenth-century western Jewry as the verse: 'I will make you a light to the nations' (49, 6). But the text became an ideological weapon in its use by Zionist and anti-Zionist. It is therefore apposite to remember that the text deals with the election of Israel. But the different election of the gentiles also

9

becomes the concern of the prophet. Cyrus is chosen as the holder of power; the priest walks through history without wielding a sword.

> 'Thus says the Lord to Cyrus his anointed . . . For the sake of Jacob my servant and Israel my chosen I have called you by name and given you your title, though you have not known me'.
>
> (Isaiah 45, 1, 4)

The Bible connects election with a vision verifying the election. The prophet's election receives its seal through a vision which makes the time and place of the election a valid historic event. Isaiah, chosen to be a prophet, has a vision of God sitting as King on his throne. Ezekiel, in the hour of his election, sees God on a *merkavah*, on a throne-carriage, driving away into the *galut* with his people Israel. The author of Isaiah 40 sees God as the home-coming God. We must consider the situation carefully. Is the message of joy of Isaiah 40 telling the world of the home-coming people or of the home-coming God? After Isaiah's vision of God as King, after Ezekiel's vision of God driving his carriage the way Israel is now journeying, we have the vision of the home-coming God. The answer to the question 'Who is coming home?' is given with the words 'Your God is here' (40, 9). This 'Your God is here' puts an end to any one-sided interpretation of the Second Book of Isaiah. It is a text which concerns the renewal of the election of the Jewish people in the Land of Israel and in 'Babylon'. Man facing history always has the good tidings: God is here.

Geiger must not, at least not exclusively, be seen as a Liberal rabbi. Hirsch must not be seen as a pre-*Shulhan Arukh* Orthodox rabbi. Both were forceful speakers of a new chapter of history, of a true Jewish renaissance in which messianism and pietism rose as powers which renewed Judaism and made a western Judaism into true Judaism.

10

II

Prophetic Judaism and the *Halachah*

Halachah *and* Sunna

No word of the Jewish vocabulary has been used as often recently as the word *halachah*. It is understood as a legal term. Because of the central place given to this term in the discussion between the Orthodox and Progressive sections of modern Jewry, the whole mass of arguments elaborated by Progressive Jewish thinkers shifted into the background, and their achievements were fogotten. What had been made articulate through doctrinal formulation was forgotten. Forgotten, too, was the successful Jewish formulation of Judaism through doctrine. Now, after the breakdown of Jewish Progressive learning owing to the cataclysmic end of the German-Jewish renaissance in the nineteenth century, Jews ignored the access to Judaism through doctrine and spoke only of *halachah*, wrongly understood as an exclusively legal term. Arguments about the Torah became arguments about a Jewish law. The dialogue between Progressives and Orthodox left the philosophical or at least the theoretical level and became instead a controversy between two or more schools of law. Even the Progressives, who could have argued with the clarified ideas and with the historical achievements of the German-Jewish past, ignored the rich treasures of that past and defended their non-Orthodox Judaism as if pleading before judges who had all the answers in their codes of law. An unthinking dogmatic use of the word *halachah* transformed our prophetic and classical rabbinic Judaism, the Judaism of Yavneh, the Judaism of Yohanan ben Zakkai, into a kind of Islam. A revived understanding of the term *halachah* and a rejection of the post-holocaust use of this term will again make Judaism the Judaism of the prophets and the tannaitic rabbis. Where this is done — and it must be done, especially in

11

Israel — the rabbis will be rabbis and not *ulema*, not officials dispensing law with religious authority.

God demands justice. This is His Law. It is absolute law, eternally valid. The laws regulating social and political life are relative laws, changeable according to circumstances.

It may seem as though Jewish and Islamic religious concepts are nowhere as near to each other as in the concept of the Hebrew word *halachah*. This assumed nearness is the very mistake which has to be rejected. *Halachah* is a noun derived from the verb *haloch*, to walk. It may seem furthermore as though this word *halachah* belongs more to the vocabulary of rabbinic than of prophetic Judaism. This is doubtful. The linguistic history of the word *halachah* begins with Micah 6, 8, where it says:

'God has told you, O man, what is good;
and what is it that the Lord asks of you?
Only to act justly, to love loyalty,
to walk wisely before your God.'

Here, in Micah's Hebrew *lechet* we have the word 'to walk'. The linguistic origin of the word *halachah* clearly points to prophetic language. What does God ask from man? The answer is: He asks man to walk a certain way. *Halachah* means 'walking'. What in Hebrew is called *halachah* is called in Arabic *sunna*, 'path', a path trodden, as it has always been trodden. We must think of the camel in the caravan. If it walks on the trodden path, it will arrive at the oasis with palm trees and life-giving water. If the trodden path is left, the way leads to death in the waterless desert. *Halachah* can be misinterpreted as being what the Muslim's *sunna* is. This misinterpretation is avoided when the prophetic meaning of *halachah* remains alive.

Man walking with God, walking before God — the translation may vary, but not the meaning — this is the Jew. To put the same point in a different way: The Jew is a man like everybody else, a man in his ordinary full humanity, but a man walking with God. The Jew is a man walking in the path of the *halachah*. A *halachah*, derived from Micah 6, 8 or from any other prophet, demands a specific deed which is always guided by only one motive: to walk with God.

12

The Jew walking the path of the *halachah* — *halachah* understood not as *sunna* but in its original meaning in the prophetic speech — is a man in his unchanged humanity. The Christian, on the other hand, is not merely a man in his ordinary human state, he is as a Christian, a 'changed man', a man who has had his encounter on the Damascus Road. Damascus makes the Christian a 'new man', 'a new Adam'. The mere humanity of man does not make a man a Christian.

The Jew walks a certain way, the Christian believes. *Halachah* versus faith, this is the difference between Jew and Christian. The Jew walks the way through history, and history has its various oases of peace and its chain of catastrophes. But the Jew walks on. The Jew walks the way before God, with God, that is to say he walks in hope. His walking before God, with God, makes his way in history a way leading to the Kingdom of God. For the Jew the Kingdom of God is not merely a doctrine. The Jew walking with God makes the Kingdom of God a reality, both to himself and to everyone who beholds him walking on. There is no solution for the Jewish question; neither assimilationist theology nor Zionism can offer one. The Jew, walking with God through history, walks on without relying on an historical solution. His way is meaningful to him as *halachah*, as a way leading to the Kingdom of God. Those who stop walking on as Jews and see no solution for the Jewish predicament of a life in the midst of the gentiles cannot be contradicted in their pessimistic view. Those who go on walking through history as Jews claim only one reason: their hope in history's progress to the Kingdom of God.

Judaism is inseparably connected with the conviction of the holiness of the moral law. The *halachah* leads the Jew into the realm of the moral law. But the *halachah* can also lead into the realm of ritual and into the socio-political order into which history places the Jew. Where *halachah* contradicts the moral law, we reject it as a misinterpreted directive and insist on a reform of the *halachah*. Jewish history is the history of a *halachah* continuously changing, continuously reformed, continuously rejected as out of date. The history of the *halachah* is a history in which it was faithfully kept and was also rigorously

13

rejected. This rejection took place without a revolution: some *halachah* was simply forgotten and in this way deleted from tradition.

Most Jewish benedictions start with the formula: 'Blessed art Thou, O Lord our God, King of the Universe, who hast sanctified us with Thy commandments . . .' This is the general introduction, after which the specific benediction follows. Judaism, we say, is a Judaism of the *mitsvot* (commandments). Judaism is not constituted by doctrines, like Christianity, it is constituted by commandments. Islam is constituted, as the Muslim would say, by the *sunna*, by the *hadith*, by tradition leading back to the Koran.

In numerous cases our Bible thunders imperatives. The Jew hears again and again the words: 'Thou shalt'. Yet the Bible is a document of antiquity, and we must not expect in it an orderly system which separates moral laws from laws concerning rituals and from laws which regulate the social life of the individual and the group. With the laws of the latter type historical relativity creeps into the text of our Holy Writ, in which we rightly search for and read of the eternal, unchangeable moral law. When we obey the moral law in the many instances of our life, we are in agreement with the prophetic *halachah*, with Micah 6, 8 — 'God has told you, O man, what is good . . .' — and with similar prophetic injunctions.

By distinguishing between a prophetic and a rabbinic *halachah* we do not say that the rabbinic *halachah* is cut off from the spirit of the prophets. The rabbinic *halachah* too, must be in harmony with prophetic teaching. The rabbinic *halachah* differs from that of the prophets in the fact that the rabbis added the practical details of Jewish life to the admonition of the prophets. Only in this is there a difference between prophet and rabbi. To give an example, the prophets demanded: 'Keep the sabbath!' The rabbis showed how this is done. The prophets demanded kindness towards one's fellow man. The rabbis showed how it is done. But in each *halachah*, including the *halachah* concerned with the rituals and with conformity to social laws, there remains one motive inherent: to do the good deed, 'to walk wisely before God'. Never must a *halachah* be

14

without that motive. A *halachah* can never be anything but a moral way. An immoral *halachah* must be eradicated from both biblical and post-biblical commandments. The *halachah* 'which Moses received on Mount Sinai' — to accept this solemn formula — concerns the moral law, the one moral law, obeyed on the numerous occasions when man is a doer. A choice is before him: he can do right, or he can do wrong. He always lives under the rule of the moral law. In his obedience to this rule he obeys the *halachah* 'which Moses received on Mount Sinai'. The moral law speaks in each man's conscience. It is the categorical imperative demanding absolute obedience. 'The eternal stars above me and the moral law within me' — this Kantian formula expresses the text of Micah 6, 8, 'God has told you, O man, what is good . . .'

Why, then, has the word 'moralist' its derogatory meaning? Are not Kant and Micah and the other prophets moralists? The word 'moralist' should not be applied to these men who with so mighty a voice proclaimed the holiness of the moral law. They should not be called moralists, because the moralist does not understand the sanctity which is in forgiveness, and because he does not know the miracle of atonement. The biblical prophet and all those who follow him, rabbis and ordinary Jews, and those who read the Gospels, are not moralists when they categorically demand: 'Do what is good, and avoid what is wrong!' Like the prophets the rabbis must demand a *halachah* in strict harmony with morality, and like the priest officiating on Yom Kippur in the Temple they must preach forgiveness and atonement. From the Book of Leviticus, in which the atonement service of primordial times is described, up to the huge neon letters on a New York sky-scraper which shed the word Yom Kippur over the great city, Jews have combined their belief in atonement with their rigorous ethics. Thus Jews did not become cheerless puritans, but remained merciful in their moral way of life.

It is not merely on liberal theological grounds that the term '*halachah* of the prophet' has been introduced here. Obviously everyone using the term '*halachah*' in the usual traditional approach connects this term with a decision handed down from

15

the past to the present by a rabbi or by a rabbinical collegium. My reason for speaking of the *halachah* of the prophets has to do with an event which happened in Jewish history; indeed, in the history of mankind. This event is the new light in which our Holy Writ, the Bible, is seen in the post-medieval age. We see the Bible, the Torah, the Christian Gospels too, for that matter, as historical documents *only* and not as a kind of miraculous meteor which has fallen from heaven. The Muslim sees the Koran in this unhistorical way. He sees it as a book, but as a book incomparable to any other book. Liberal Jews and liberal Christians, or Progressive Jews and Progressive Christians — it makes no difference whether we say Liberal or Progressive — see the Hebrew Bible and also the Gospels as we see any other book: a book written by writers who, whatever they were, were human beings. This is the effect which historical criticism has on our post-medieval generation. The authority of the Bible or of the Gospels is not impugned by this. The authority of the Bible and of the Gospels is the authority of men, but of men with a mission, a mission still meaningful for us today. This authority is that of the prophet. The prophet, this man who is not a superman, speaks and the word he speaks is the word of God. To quote Franz Rosenzweig: 'The ways of God and the ways of man are different. But the word of God and the word of man are the same.' Man can speak, can write down what he says, and what he speaks and what he writes down are the words of God. Man can be a prophet.

We need not be afraid or puzzled at the question: What is our *Tenach,* our Hebrew Bible? The question, put in the traditional form: 'What does the Torah say?' can be asked and can be answered. Our Torah is a book written by men. Those who wrote our Holy Scripture are men, who are lawyers, psalmists and chroniclers; above all they are prophets. What was possible in the past is possible in our contemporary history. Mohammed regarded himself as the 'last prophet'. This separates him as a heretic from both Judaism and Christianity. The prophet speaks and makes his demands in any contemporary history.

The rabbinic *halachah* is justified through tradition. With the *halachah* of the prophet it is different. The prophet need not

16

fall back on tradition for the justification of his message. His own personal conviction makes his message a prophetic message. The words in which he transmits his message to those who do and to those who do not want to listen to it start with the introduction: 'Thus speaks the Lord.' Men like Rashi (1040–1105) and other medieval commentators did not understand what a prophet is. We do understand the prophet. We listen to the 'thou shalt' speaking in man's conscience . Listening to the voice of moral conscience we walk, as the *halachah* of Micah 6, 8 demands, before God. We are able to revive, to reform and also to reject any *halachah*. In this way we arrive at a *halachah* rightly described as '*halachah* of the prophet' and abolish the distinction between halachic and prophetic Judaism.

The battle for the rehabilitation of the rabbi was fought in the nineteenth century in the theological seminaries and in the universities. There the rabbi of the past — the Pharisee of the New Testament — was at last shown to be an equal of the prophet. The historians dealing with the century in which the Gospels were written had to admit that Judaism is both prophetic and rabbinic Judaism. This victory has lost its relevance to the rabbinic Judaism of the present time. The Orthodox rabbis in Israel and in diaspora Jewry today are not equals of the prophets. They are more like the *ulema* of Islam. Their *halachah* is based on antiquated tradition, not on prophetic conviction. A revival of Judaism will make it necessary to refer again to the controversy which once existed between the Pharisee as the Gospels saw him and the Pharisee of the tannaitic rabbinate. Today it is the controversy in which rabbis have to stop being what the *ulema* are: officials without the courage of a prophetic interpretation of a past tradition. Orthodox rabbis must be told that their *halachah* is the Islamic *sunna*.

Jewish Orthodoxy as Islamised Judaism
The way in which we understand the word Torah and in which we translate the Hebrew word into a word of our western world is of great significance. In Anglo-Jewry and, following Anglo-

17

Jewry, in Israel and in other places of the diaspora, Torah is often translated as '(Jewish) law'. In this translation of Torah, Torah is in principle made equal to, say, Roman law or English law, in short, to any law of a State. Yet any demanding word of a prophet is Torah. Torah can mean law, as it can mean guidance through doctrinal teaching. When Torah means law, it must not be reduced to a particular law, excluding the many applications to the situations of mankind. Torah understood as 'Jewish law' is reduced to a document, a book which lies conveniently on the table, to be used by a lawyer in his arguments. But the Torah is not a book, as is the Koran.

Torah as law is universal law. Its universality makes it equal with love because it concerns the whole of mankind: law and love cease to be contradictions. A particular law, on the other hand, demands obedience in the way in which Allah has to be obeyed. The Muslim must obey Allah, but is not expected to love him. A sermon on the text 'God is love' does not fit into the atmosphere of a mosque. Allah is merciful, but except in Sufism he is not imagined as a loving God, who is more forgiving than punishing. This religious situation is mirrored in the everyday life of the Muslim. Marriage-law and poetry reveal the Muslim as a responsible husband but not really as a lover.

To speak of the Torah as 'Jewish law' shows the deep penetration of Islam into Judaism. To struggle for a revival of classical, i.e. prophetic, Judaism, means to reject Islamised Judaism. To see the Torah as 'Jewish law', as only relevant to the particular realm of Jewish life, and to be blind to the universal relevance of the Torah to mankind is what we call its Islamisation. But Islam is monotheism without prophecy. To understand the Torah as 'Jewish law', as is the way of Jewish Orthodoxy, means to reduce it to a Judaism without prophecy.

The Orthodox rabbis of today reveal themselves as clerics, who are not rabbis but *ulema*. These '*ulema*–rabbis' teach that Torah means 'Jewish law', written and eternally unchangeable. Man can run away from it, but he cannot change it. This view of Jewish law is mistaken. With the prophetic element in Judaism alive, Jewish law can be changed. The term 'oral law' is only a legal fiction without a basis in history to sustain it, but it

18

expresses the possibility that laws can be changed, and even new laws can be added to the bulk of previous ones, the so-called 'written laws'.

With the prophetic element in Judaism alive, Jewish laws can be changed. With the prophetic character alive in a rabbi, he knows what can and what cannot be changed. He knows that with the progress from the Middle Ages into the modern western world a lot has to be changed. He also knows that Torah identified with moral law remains unchangeable.

With the slogan the Torah is 'Jewish law' the Orthodox rabbi changes our Jewish monotheistic community into a monolithic organisation, and the Torah itself is changed into a political ideology. The Torah viewed as 'Jewish law' becomes what the flag of the State is to the citizen-soldier. He must not desert the flag. Right or wrong, its command has to be obeyed. The Torah become 'Jewish law' robs the 'Citizens of Yavneh' of their freedom, makes them a mute part of a totalitarian system.

In Judaism two elements have to be alive: prophecy and piety. Living Judaism is sustained by both prophet and priest. Both these religious types have to influence Jewish life. The prophet speaks the word of God. He speaks a demanding word, but he is not a lawgiver. The sad result of a diagnosis of contemporary Jewry shows it as a pious community; pious, but without a sense of prophetic reaction to the events of its time. They are *froom*, but solely *froom*. On the other hand, everybody who speaks up against a petrified Judaism and brings forward sound propostions leading to a revival not only displays piety but represents today those human qualities which made the prophet of biblical times a prophet. It goes without saying that with the prophet on the stage of history the false prophet too has to be reckoned with. But this is the price we have to pay for a history in which the prophetic controversy regains its creative power. Above all, the prophet must not be put on such a high pedestal that he is unthinkable in the human society of our day. Franz Rosenzweig described the prophet walking among us and talking to us in our democratic era. Rosenzweig's description of prophecy is both monumental and simple. 'The ways of God are different from the ways of man, but the word of God

19

and the word of man are the same. What man hears in his heart as his own human speech is the very word which comes out of God's mouth.' Commenting on Rosenzweig we can say: 'Listen to what man says to man, and you will hear the word of God.' Rosenzweig's description of prophecy — the word of God is a word spoken by man — is also expressed in Deuteronomy 30, 11-14: 'The commandment that I lay on you this day is not too difficult for you, it is not too remote. It is not in heaven, that you should say, "Who will go up to heaven for us to fetch it and tell it to us, so that we can keep it?" Nor is it beyond the sea, that you should say, "Who will cross the sea for us to fetch it and tell it to us, so that we can keep it?" It is a thing very near to you, upon your lips and in your heart ready to be kept.'

The Torah, the word of God become a written document, become a book — this is Islam. The word of God, become 'flesh', a Church, a civilization — this is Christianity. The word of God spoken by man to man — this is Judaism. When the word God is no longer understood as addressed to man by man, but seen as enshrined in an unchangeable code, the Torah ceases to be the Torah of the prophets.

With the slogan 'The Torah is "Jewish law" ', the theologically uneducated, *Yeshiva*-trained rabbis drive away the intellectual and do not let his contribution, his 'oral law', become part of the dialogue in which the word of God is heard. The *ulema* and the *ulema*-rabbis both say: 'If you take a single stone out of the edifice of the Torah, of the *sunna*, the whole edifice will fall down.' Torah understood like the *sunna* of the Muslim — this is the teaching of the Orthodox rabbi of today. Jewish Orthodoxy is Judaism Islamised.

Judaism is not only in danger of becoming Islamised, it is also in danger of becoming Christianised. During the last two centuries continental Jewry was exposed to and in danger of assimilating to Pauline and Johannine Christianity.* In the Anglo-Saxon world Petrine Christianity influenced Jews too weak to resist assimilation. Petrine Christianity, more than Pauline and Johannine Christianity, affirms law as part of Christianity. The result is a Christian shaped by his devotion to

*See I. Maybaum, *Jewish Existence* (London, 1960), pp. 153 ff., *Trialogue*, pp. 108 ff.

20

law. No antinomianism for the Petrine Christian! Assimilation
to British surroundings creates a Jewish type willing to obey the
law. The strange situation arises in which Jews who in fact live
outside Jewish life uncritically respect the standards of Jewish
Orthodoxy. They do not live the life of Orthodox Jews and are
in this respect absolute outsiders, but neither do they participate in a programme of reform, in any prophetic attempt at
change: it would be against 'the law'. These non-Jewish Jews
object to progress in Jewish religious life and display loyalty to
orthodox established forms. The petrified details of the tradition are, as they say, 'the law'. 'Is that the law?', Shylock asks in
humility (*The Merchant of Venice*, Act 4, Scene 1). Shylock's
belief in the validity of the law, even an absurd law, is tragic.
But the situation can change from tragedy to comedy, showing
a non-Orthodox Jew in Anglo-Jewry as a defender of
Orthodoxy. He claims to be Orthodox and joins the rank and
file of Orthodox groups. A Jew, assimilated to Anglo-Saxon
surroundings, himself a non-practising Jew, defends the old
petrified tradition more with upper-class snobbishness than
with Shylock's humility. 'Nothing can be done, nothing must
be done,' say the Jewish gentlemen confessing Jewish
Orthodoxy. The 'law' makes any redeeming action impossible.
In this case it is not Islamised but Christianised Judaism which
causes soulless stagnation.

Atrophy of Morality in Halachic Judaism
Today *halachah* can very well be defined as legality. There is a
law of some kind. Obedience to this law produces an action.
The motive for this action does not play any part in its performance. The main thing on this level of activity is the result. I may
give alms to a needy person in order to get rid of the annoying
picture of distress. On the other hand I may act differently: I
give my bit to the needy out of charity. The result in both cases
seems to be identical. But something very important makes the
actions very different: the motive.

Whether an action is in truth a moral action depends on its
motive. An action performed out of unreflecting obedience to a

21

law, military obedience for instance, is without the splendour of morality. As an action on the level of mere legality something has been done because it had to be done. It was done because 'the Joneses did it', or because it had always been done. It was done because of legal obligation. The heart and soul of a moral motive is missing.

All this amounts to a weakness inherent in a Judaism reduced to one-sided halachic order. *Halachah* demands obedience only in the field of legal activity. The motive alone can make an action performed according to the *halachah*, indeed any action, a moral action. In a Judaism which consists entirely of halachic precepts the absence of consideration of a motive can lead to an atrophy of morality, of moral thinking and of moral practice.

Atrophy is the dangerous disease in which, say, a limb of the human body wastes away because it has not been used for a length of time. The same can happen to men's character. If action with negligence of its motive has lasted for a long time, in the end the sense of moral motive dies. If you teach a generation that mere legality suffices, moral cripples will grow up who will become convinced that the highest principle is not to be caught.

Numerous examples exist where rituals can be carried out mechanically.* What kind of a man will a child grow up to be who is told that he is permitted to listen to the wireless on *shabbat*, provided somebody else, but not he himself, has switched it on?

Halachic precepts leave no choice. They have to be obeyed. In this the *halachah* is equal to a political order. The command shouted to a platoon by the sergeant major has the same political character. The *halachah* is formulated like a political order, and it makes the Jew stand like a recruit before his sergeant major. No room is left for argument. No freedom exists to choose the form of obedience. Obedience to the *halachah* is obedience without freedom, whereas moral actions presuppose freedom. Obedience to the *halachah* is legality in slavish submission. The Muslim calls himself 'slave of God', and performs the deeds which he is obliged to do in an obedience which is identical with halachic legality. When Liberal and Reform Judaism teach that

*See *Trialogue*, p. 37.

22

'The *halachah* must not be dictated, it must be taught', the door to an end of halachic legality has been opened. The urgency of this emancipation from halachic Judaism in Israel and in the diaspora cannot be stressed enough. A medieval rabbinate robs the population of the religious freedom which every citizen in the west possesses as a matter of course.

Halachic Judaism, as mechanical legality which neglects motive, is as medieval as was the sale of letters of indulgence by the Roman Catholic Church in the Middle Ages. Halachic legality and the trade in letters of indulgence expects religious and moral effects from mere mechanical means. 'When the coin is in the box, the soul is redeemed.' This is the very magical materialism which expects action without any participation of the moral motive to be pleasing to God.

The people which has given birth to Einstein, to Franz Rosenzweig, to a score of great inventors, scholars and Nobel prizewinners, is in danger of becoming — primitive. Judaism a primitive religion? With the loss of our élite it can come to this. With the neglect and the very absence of the moral motive in a merely legalistic approach to actions a vacuum makes itself felt. The Jew may say his prayers according to the *halachah*. But if the motive for his prayer is not considered, phylacteries are supposed to fill the vacuum. The dull element in worship performed only in obedience to the *halachah* does not become less dull through wearing phylacteries. The phylacteries make Jewish prayer the worship of a primitive religion. The medieval Jew was not aware of this primitivity. After all, he was a medieval man. But for the post-medieval Jew phylacteries cannot but appear as a medieval device for the attainment of religious aims.

The great achievement of the historians of the *Wissenschaft des Judentums* school was the rehabilitation of the Pharisees. They were rabbis, different from the prophets but not in any way of less dignity. Judaism is the Judaism of the prophets and of the Pharisees, the Judaism of the prophets and the rabbis. The words of abuse in the New Testament against the Pharisees are now recognized not as a rejection which condemns the very office of the rabbi but as criticism to which individual rabbis can be subjected. The New Testament writer, in his invective against the rabbis, is like a pamphleteer, from whom historical objectivity is not to be expected. The Pharisee is not an impostor, but he can become one. No office is safe against the individual who misuses it. The rabbi can be a saintly scholar or a foolish holder of a clerical living.

The historian must beware of becoming an apologist. The historians of the *Wissenschaft des Judentums*, in rehabilitating the rabbis, performed an important task, which has changed our view of Jewish — and for that matter of Christian — history. The Pharisee, whether called rabbi or not, now stands before our eyes as different from and equal to the prophet. The New Testament, in referring to the Pharisees, records contemporary history. In this history the rabbis were what man always is in history: either rising to the height of his mission or abysmally failing in his holy duties. Above all, the *halachah* is not always the same *halachah*. The *halachah* as Rabbi Yohanan ben Zakkai saw it in the year 70 is different from the *halachah* of those codifying rabbis who went to work after the code of the *Shulhan Arukh* was written. It is therefore apposite to distinguish between the *halachah* of the classical rabbis and the *halachah* of a time which was without any creative element. The *halachah* has a history, in which there are some rabbis who successfully defend their intellectual freedom and other rabbis who are men of decadent periods, in which scholarly activity is reduced to writing commentaries to commentaries.

Today the Orthodox rabbinate in Israel and in the diaspora is without the prophetic element which should still be alive in their office. The rabbi, without any spark of prophetic Judaism, snatching power for himself from the State, is not a true servant of the Jewish people. There are, of course, righteous men who serve as rabbis and are rightly revered by their flocks. But there is also the unfortunate fact of a rabbinate wielding power. This unfortunate fact of State and Religion not being properly separated deprives the Jewish people in Israel and even in the diaspora of freedom. The words of abuse which in the New Testament are hurled against rabbis, who are called hypocrites and other ugly names, are not invalidated by the

24

rehabilitation of the Pharisees which has taken place. The Orthodox rabbi can be the very type which is condemned in the New Testament, and no less severely in Jewish writing too. Israel is plagued with the 'lawyers and Pharisees' of Matthew 23.

But there is hope. Rabbis of the Progressive Movement, Liberal and Reform rabbis, can show the way to the understanding of Judaism.

New Names for the Torah (The Torah Demythologised)

A new age creates new names, and these make history a meaningful course of events which man is capable of understanding. God brought all the animals and birds 'to the man to see what he would call them, and whatever the man called each living creature, that was its name' (Genesis 2, 19). But man is not only a namegiver in nature, in this way he is also creative in history.

Contemporary man cannot but call the Enlightenment Movement one of the greatest events of which he knows. It still lives on in our scientific age. For three thousand years before the Enlightenment Jews spoke of the Torah. After the Enlightenment, they introduced a new name for the word Torah: they spoke of 'Judaism'.

Jews had begun to look at what they had uncritically called Torah with the critical eye of the scientific historian. With historical criticism becoming the general approach of scholars, the Torah was regarded like any work of world literature. It had evidently been written, as the works of Goethe and Shakespeare had been written. But where were the uniqueness and the holiness of the Torah? The word Judaism entered the consciousness of post-medieval man as the rescuing force. It expressed what the word Torah had expressed before. The new word Judaism made the Torah one of the monotheistic world religions. With the Torah called Judaism and set high on the pedestal of a universal world religion nothing was lost. So it seemed. The Jew, affirming the truth and the holiness of the Torah, was faithful to the truth and holiness enshrined in the world religion called Judaism. With the replacement of the word Torah by the word Judaism a discussion started in which contemporary Jewry is still involved. This discussion began with Moses Mendelssohn. It leads on to Franz Rosenzweig. A passionate search for the right attribute for the new word Judaism became the content of post-medieval Jewish history. Which attribute could make it clear that Judaism preserved the truth and holiness which the word Torah had contained? Among the various attributes added to the word Judaism, 'Prophetic Judaism' proved to express in modern Jewry what the word Torah had meant to Jews for three thousand years.

Between Mendelssohn and Rosenzweig stand a score of men, rabbis, theologians and historians, whose memory has to be blessed for their contribution to our lives as Jews. These men with their liberal belief helped us in a decided way to preserve our Jewish status after the Middle Ages had gone. But we shall not offer biographies. Biographies end up in legends. Men become mythologised, whereas events which indicate a new era disappear from sight in the lumber of history. True, legends are dear to us, and they have much to teach us. But when all is taken into account, our exposition will be less a biography and more a linguistic analysis of new names given to the Torah in the age beginning with the Enlightenment Movement and leading up to our own day. In the linguistic philosophy of which Rosenzweig was a pioneer words do not merely signify abstract information, they are a semantic means creating a revelatory dialogue between the one who speaks and the one who listens. The words under discussion in the following passages are: Reform Judaism, Historical Judaism, Liberal Judaism, Orthodoxy and tradition. In contrast to what all these new words stand for we have also to speak of politicised Judaism.

Among the new names, the name Reform was the first to appear. It recommended itself as expressing what had happened both in the world at large and in Jewish life: the end of the Middle Ages. But was the word Enlightenment not more appropriate for Jews? Reform, and even more Reformation, points to Luther and to an entirely Christian history. Enlightenment implies reason, science, progress, freedom.

At the Rabbinical Assemblies of 1844–48 Reform was opposed by men who in arguing their case used a further new name for the Torah: Historical Judaism. This means that the antagonism between Enlightenment and Romanticism invaded the Jewish scene. The Jew as Romantic, as conservative defender of the Middle Ages, as opponent of progress — what a farce! The Jew got his freedom, his emancipation, from those who fought the Middle Ages. Poets and dreamers may paint a rosy picture of the Middle Ages. The truth is different: dirt, drunkenness, prostitution, cruelty were more evident in the medieval city than knights, ladies, troubadours and saintly priests. The stinking cities harboured all kinds of disease. The castles, which might seem a picturesque sight to the tourists of today, were in their time dungeons in which prisoners languished until they were ransomed for cash. The Middle Ages in Poland were even more barbaric than they were in the west. But it is exactly the attire of the Polish Middle Ages that the group led by the Lubavitch Guru wish to preserve. These champions of Conservative Judaism wear Polish headgear. Anglo-Saxon Liberalism tolerates these pious fools who walk in the ghettos of London and New York like an alien army from a far-off world, exhibiting themselves as remnants of the long defunct Polish feudal world.

The most careful criticism has to be applied when the word 'Historical Judaism' is used. What was meant a hundred years ago by 'Historical Judaism', might be today expressed by the word 'Conservative Judaism'. We must distinguish between the three monotheistic religions in respect of their attitude to revelation and messianism. 'Sinai' stands for revelation. Each generation stands, indeed must stand, before 'Sinai'. Time is pregnant with messianic possibility. The Messiah stands round the corner. He might usher in redemption today. So far Judaism. For the Christian it is different. For him revelation has happened, and it has happened at one point in history, at one point only, at Golgotha, and on one specific date, in the year one. The Christian does not, like the Jew, still wait for the Messiah. Christian belief has the message of a Messiah who has arrived. The Muslim with his creed of Mohammed as the last

Messiah cuts himself off from a history understood as a messianic movement.

All this has practical consequences and makes Jew, Christian and Muslim act differently in history. The Jew waits in messianic expectation. 'Happy the man who waits' (Daniel 12, 12). The Jew wanders through history in hope. Glory to the Eternal Way! The Christian contemplates an event which stands still and is infused with spiritual splendour. A Messiah, a God-man, has been born. A revolution changes history in one single event. The Muslim sees history as terrestrial eternity. Time stands still, and change is rebellion. There is a path, the *sunna*, to diverge from which means heading for catastrophe. The Muslim has no trust in history, he does not even have a concept of it.

Now we are able to judge whether the words 'Conservative Judaism' are an attribute applicable to the Torah. The answer must be no. Conservative man may often be faithful to a sound inherited tradition in day-to-day affairs. But the word tradition needs to be understood theologically. With the word tradition we opt for a religious decision which forbids us, for instance, to denigrate the Middle Ages. Above all with the programme of a Conservative Judaism we leave the world about which the prophets preached. Prophetic Judaism is not Conservative Judaism. Prophetic Judaism upholds the messianic character of Judaism. Conservative Judaism implies the belief in stopping the flow of time, which is always of messianic character, for the sake of political expendiency. Certainly, at some time some prophets found it necessary to give advice of a conservative nature. But this does not make the prophet an opponent of progress. As a prophet he stands against the king of his time. The king represents the State. The State is safe when it is not affected by change. This makes the prophet with his vision of a time still to come the principal opponent of the State.

Some of the new words enumerated above may not intend to ascribe theological or political attributes to Judaism. They may rather point to the liturgical character of the Synagogue service. This may contain nostalgically preserved rituals from the past or a courageously introduced new way of worship. These differences may irritate the rank and file of a congregation but

28

need not concern important issues. For one who can pray, for one who is of such a frame of mind that he feels he must pray, the question whether to pray in the way of his grandfathers or in a way which commends itself through its style to a new generation does not constitute a truly profound religious division. What creates a serious division in our present generation is the politicisation of Jewish thinking and, connected with it, the denial of freedom by Jews to Jews. In Israel State power is in the hands of rabbis, and in the diaspora the establishment of rabbinical courts makes rabbis officials who exercise power when it comes to marital matters and to proselytisation. A rabbi in possession of power — this is the end of Prophetic Judaism, indeed the end of Judaism. Modern Judaism needs a revival of Liberal Judaism. Liberal Judaism goes back to the days of the Enlightenment Movement, which liberated us from the Middle Ages. After the cataclysmic events of our time a second emancipation has to be initiated.

Liberal Judaism must rise from its present inertia, must aim at a revival of the spirit which made Franz Rosenzweig announce to his generation 'I am a Liberal', and must fight for reason, freedom and progress.

Two new names substituted for the word Torah can guide us out of the darkness in which our generation lives at present: Liberal Judaism and Prophetic Judaism. The word Liberal Judaism opens the door for what Prophetic Judaism stands for.

Christian theologians have made the prophet a saint, a miracle-man, a soothsayer. The prophet is a man who speaks, and the words he speaks turn out to be the word of God. Liberalism, unlike socialism and nationalism, leads to man himself and to him alone. In Liberalism it is man, not a collective group or utopian aim, that is in the centre. This makes Liberalism, albeit a political ideology, free to be the basis for Prophetic Judaism. In Prophetic Judaism as in political liberalism it is man who speaks. In our days the question 'Who is a Jew?' has proved to be impossible to answer satisfactorily. For this question to be answered, the question 'What is man?' has to be answered first. Man is a speaker of words. In this capacity he reaches his peak. The word of God is a word spoken by man.

29

The prophet speaks it. The revival of Prophetic Judaism demands the return of man to our private world. Man, being nothing else but man, will tell us what is justice and mercy and holiness. A revival of Judaism will be preceded by a revival of the understanding of man. Everything which we cherish between heaven and earth has its source in man. The way to God begins in man — or, to use a biblical phrase, it is the wrestling of man with God. Liberalism, restoring man to his exalted place, can, of course, like any form of humanism, become a self-sufficient philosophy and deprive itself of the possibility of transcending from our here and now to God. But Liberalism and humanism can ascend to the heights where we face God. This makes Liberalism the philosophical and political condition for Prophetic Judaism. Liberalism and humanism are not identical with Prophetic Judaism. But Liberalism and humanism are reliable 'carriers' (in Karl Becker's phrase) of Prophetic Judaism.

Conversion to Judaism is seen by Orthodox rabbis in racial terms. The very word conversion should have no place in the world of Jewish thought. Conversion is a Christian experience. It leads man to the road to Damascus, and thus makes him a Christian, a changed man, a 'new Adam'. No conversion exists in this form in Judaism, and therefore no ritual can be stipulated for it. No ritual needs to be searched for. The *mikvah*, the ritual bath which is supposed, as it were, with magical power to change a person, to make him fit for his entry into the House of Israel, should be seen in its primitivity. To join the Jewish prayer community and the Jewish brotherhood means to walk with those who take it upon themselves to carry the yoke of the Kingdom of God. This is an enterprise involving persecution. About this the newcomer must be clear. But what enables anyone to join the House of Israel is the image of God in man. Anyone can become a Jew, without further conditions, because he is a man.

In pursuing Prophetic Judaism we have to oppose politicised Judaism. In politicised Judaism different words from those scrutinised in this chapter have to be faced, and they will be discussed in the following chapters.

30

Western Jewry has to emancipate itself from the consequences of its politicisation. The main controversy of contemporary Judaism is between a so-called Liberalism and a so-called
Orthodoxy. From the start we must see Liberalism as a political
movement. But its involvement with Christianity has again to
be recognised. Jewish Orthodoxy has to be recognised as being
culturally penetrated by Islam (see *Trialogue*, p. 44 and p. 115).
In the fog of the various ideologies of politicised modern Jewry
the great impact of Christianity and Islam on Judaism has to be
discovered. The Liberal Jew often argues with the help of
Christian doctrines, the Orthodox Jew as an Islamised Jew.
Theological thinking has to clear the air. The western Jew
cannot avoid using Christian doctrines, the non-westernised
Jew cannot avoid accepting a form of life which is shaped by the
imam and not by the rabbi. There is no harm in this, as long as
we call a spade a spade, as long as we see when Christianity and
Islam are grafted onto Judaism. What is urgently needed is a
rediscovery of Prophetic Judaism. This will transform the confrontation between the three monotheistic religions into a creative trialogue. It will transform politicised Judaism into
Prophetic Judaism. Ideology will be replaced by theology.

III

Implications of Citizenship

The Citizens of Yavneh
THE destruction of the Temple in Jerusalem by the Romans in
the year 70 is not merely a date of Jewish history. It concerns the
whole of mankind. This date records the confrontation between
East and West, between State and monotheism. This cataclysmic event of Jewish history still occupies the mind of men
all over the globe. Two new institutions, the Synagogue and the
Church, arose at the side of the Roman Empire, i.e. at the side
of the secular State, the 'naked State', whether glorified or
cursed.

Rabbi Yohanan ben Zakkai left the battle area, where the
zealots were fighting the Roman soldiers. He asked the Roman
general for permission to establish a community in Yavneh,
where Jews could live according to the Jewish calendar. The
request of the rabbi was granted. It was not a pietistic (hasidic)
exodus from history that the rabbi had in mind. He aimed at an
exodus from gentile history. With his calendar the Jew lives in
the cycle in which the eternally unchanging events of Creation
and Exodus are commemorated. The commemoration of these
events, be it written or oral, be it formulated as commandments
to be obeyed or as doctrines to be accepted as true, is the content
of the Torah. The Torah integrates the eternally unchanging
cycle of the Jewish calendar into the whole way of life of the
Jew.

Yavneh is the archetype of that community which the Jew
needs for the sake of his survival. Yavneh is not a Jewish State.
But it has the capacity of cooperating with the State. Seen from
a purely political perspective Rabbi Yohanan ben Zakkai is a
traitor. As such he appears to the zealots of all times. The
zealots devote everything they have to their State. What the

32

rabbis discussed as free men in the Talmud was established in Yavneh. With Rabbi Yohanan's Yavneh the Jewish people could exist in the Roman era as a people dispersed all over the Mediterranean basin. With Yavneh Jewish life under the conditions of the diaspora was established.

The Christian politician, too, has his 'Yavneh', but not in the same way as the Jewish people. The 'Christian Yavneh' becomes established with the help of a division between spiritual and secular. The Christian must rise into the spiritual sphere in order to become a Christian. The Church is a spiritual Yavneh. The Christian politician promises the Caesar always to remain aware of his obligation to a dual loyalty created by two authorities: God and Caesar. With the year 70 begins the era of Yavneh and also the epoch of the Christian era.

As 'citizens of Yavneh' we were closely connected with the realm of the Romans and also with Christian civilization. Obviously our Jewish historians took note of that. But they have only lately taken note of the great impact of Islamic civilization on the Jewish people. Eastern European Jewry, Jewry seen with romantic spectacles by the writer Sholem Aleichem, is now seen to be part of Mediterranean Islamic civilization. Julius Caesar is a Mediterranean man. So is Rabbi Akiba. So is the Jew of the Continental diaspora. The Turks besieged and nearly conquered Vienna. The historian of ideas with his linguistic microscope reveals the hitherto unnoticed fact that the Yiddish-speaking Jew of Eastern Europe and the Arabic-speaking Jew in the Mediterranean basin are both shaped by Islamic influence. Up to the influx of the ideas of emancipation, the Jew is a Mediterranean man. But in Israel he is a Mediterranean man no longer. The Jew was able to create the State of Israel because he had become a westerner.

We can point to the exact moment when the Mediterranean world ceased to be the place of rich creative activity and became the sterile and stagnating Levant. Bronowski, in his lectures *The Ascent of Man*, shows convincingly that the brute force of the Christian Church in making Galileo recant his Copernican theory caused the end of the freedom necessary for creative work, for science and progress. The ecclesiastical judges in the trial of Galileo, which affected the fate of mankind, argued with biblical texts about matters of science. Galileo argued from insight he had gained through observation and experience. After Galileo the creative spirit which had enriched the Mediterranean basin ceased to contribute new ideas, and history moved away to the north. Spinoza and Leibniz are the men of progressing history. The judges of Galileo believed that truth should dominate, Galileo believed that truth should persuade. At his trial Galileo faced a pope, cardinals and other high dignitaries of the Church. But we must not be deceived by appearances. The Pope condemning Galileo acted like a Muslim judge. He used State power to crush a dissident believer. The Inquisition, outwardly a Christian institution, was no longer thinking and acting according to Christian spirituality. The official wearing the priestly robes of the Christian Church in fact acted like a Muslim.

The rabbi in his fight against the Karaites has to be viewed in the same way. The Torah which excludes the possibility of change is a Koran. The controversy between the Karaites and the rabbis shows them as not different from each other. Both insisted that the *halachah*, the legal formulation of the Torah, should be dictated. In fact, it should be taught. The halachist gives his answers (responsa) to questions. The answers are meekly accepted and no longer discussed. The rabbi as *gaon*, as a man in possession of unquestioned authority in the interpretation of the law, points to the beginning of the sickness of Mediterranean Jewry and eventually to the lack of new ideas in Sephardic Jewry. Sephardic Jewish literature becomes a series of commentaries to commentaries. The *Shulhan Arukh* and the commentaries around it merely serve as guides for behaviour — for forms and rituals. The gaonic period mirrored in the responsa literature shows the Jewish people in proximity to Islam. But we should not speak uncritically of an Islamic-Jewish renaissance. Rather we must recognize a Jewish assimilation to Islam, but one without a creative element on the side of the Jews. When law is reduced to a mere regulative function of ordering life, in our case Jewish in uniformity with Muslim life, Jewish monotheism is no longer true ethical monotheism.

The code has formulated its finding. This is the end of the matter. Who won, the Karaites or the rabbis? Both are losers. Both initiate the sterility of the Sephardic centuries.

The work of Maimonides suffered from this medieval throttling of freedom of thought. He laid down the content of his views in two books, in *The Guide to the Perplexed* and in his *Yad ha-Hazakah*. The first was a free discourse on the reigning philosophies of the age and their confrontation with Judaism, the second pursued the same aim in legal formulation. The first word was ostracised and branded as heretical literature, the second work fared better. It was permitted for study, because it was a legal code. The codifying rabbis of the age wanted legal finality.

Freedom returned to the Jewish people when in Berlin Moses Mendelssohn and his pupils taught historical criticism and reason as elements of Judaism. German Jewry and Eastern European Jewry went different ways. The former became a western Jewry, the latter continued in the ways of Mediterranean civilization with its adherence to the Islamic concept of law. The symbiosis of Jew and Muslim in Spain and North Africa has been hailed as a splendid renaissance. It certainly was one in many respects. But when the Emancipation formulated its aims, the foremost target was emancipation from the Islamic concept of law. The Torah is not an inflexible law. The Torah must be interpreted in its creative adaptation to new historical situations.

Diaspora and Holy Land

In the letters of Martin Buber we read of his attempt to win Stefan Zweig over to the Zionist camp. Zweig's argument rejecting Buber's invitation deserves to be quoted and preserved as precious advice for our own and a future generation. Stefan Zweig writes: 'I love the diaspora.'

The voice praising the diaspora has been silent for the last fifty years. It has been silenced. We shall turn to Isaiah, Judah ha-Levi and Franz Rosenzweig to understand why Jews could be of such a frame of mind as to love the diaspora. Is not the diaspora the life of the Jewish people in the *galut*? *Galut* means exile. Exile means being away from home. Can there be a Jewish home in the *galut*? There often has been.

The words Holy Land demand a clarification of the word holy. We have three possibilities of using this word. We can speak of spiritual holiness, of terrestrial holiness and of universal holiness. The last is expressed in Isaiah's holy: 'Holy, holy, holy is the Lord of hosts, the whole earth is full of his glory' (6, 3).

The unconsummated love of Kierkegaard for his bride Regina is spiritually holy. He loved her but would not consummate his love in marriage. His love is spiritual. The Holy Land has its spiritual holiness. In his involvement in history man always experiences an unconsummated love. We make our sacrifices for historic goals, only to find out that we cannot finish the task we set ourselves with such passion. History is full of endeavours which create islands to be revered like a Holy Land. Here Jesus was crucified, here the many crosses stood on which Alexander Yannai crucified the Pharisees. Here stood the Temple of which only the Western Wall is left. Everywhere are the memorials witnessing the many places in history which appertain to a Holy Land. History has its stories of unconsummated love. Spiritual holiness is present in history.

Palestine is a term of the geographer. The Holy Land is both a geographical term and a phrase transporting us into the realm of holiness. Whether we are Jews, Christians or Muslims, the words Holy Land are and will remain meaningful to us. But a change has occurred. Like many Jews in the Middle Ages and even later Judah ha-Levi wanted to be buried in the Holy Land. This desire is not experienced with religious intensity by post-medieval Jews, if it is experienced at all. As staunch nationalists Israelis want to *live* in Israel, and nobody in the *Secular City* gives much thought to death.

The whole history of man has its spiritual meaning. History is the story of unconsummated love, of the unfinished journey, of the promised but not fulfilled redemption. Our life is longing for the Holy Land not yet reached. Where spiritual, i.e. unconsummated, love burns with its self-fed fire, man will journey as

36

pilgrim to his Holy Land. But it is also true that it is the Christian, more than the Muslim and the Jew, for whom a pilgrimage to the Holy Land is at the very centre of his monotheism. The Christian is a crusader surging forward towards the Holy Land.

For the Muslim it is not spiritual but terrestrial holiness which moves him most. Mecca is a city. Yet it is a city in which the Muslim experiences terrestrial holiness. To him it is a holy city. In the age of nationalism, however, any capital city can appear as a Mecca. The nations awakening to stand at the side of the old nations insist on having their capital city, their Mecca, an earthly place, but in their eyes imbued with terrestrial holiness. It is not only cities that can rise into the light of terrestrial holiness. Terrestrial holiness can surround the grave of a saint or the remaining stones of the Herodian Temple. Not only the Muslim, but also the Jew and the Christian, opens his heart to the *mysterium tremendum et fascinosum* of terrestrial holiness. Judah ha-Levi unwillingly has to stop his journey to the Holy Land owing to a caprice of a stormy sea and finds himself in Egypt. He is moved at the sight of the Nile, at the sight of the place where long ago his ancestors dwelled. He, the Jew, is moved by terrestrial holiness as I was moved when, after World War II, I came back to Germany and saw again the river Rhine on the banks of which many Jewish settlements had flourished and had also met holy martyrdom. Terrestrial holiness, though characteristic of Islamic piety, can very well enter the understanding of Christian and Jew. We must not look down with sophisticated comtempt on the Jew who kisses the stones of the Western Wall. This Jew, though ignorant, stands there like a Muslim, face to face with holiness.

Where the Jew is truly a Jew and not following the Christian fascination with spiritual holiness or the Muslim fascination with terrestrial holiness, he praises God with the words of Isaiah: 'Holy, holy, holy is the Lord of Hosts: the whole earth is full of his glory.' Isaiah is not merely fascinated by the holiness rightly attributed to land or city, to spirit or matter, to any particular memorial of history or nature: he worships the Holy God. There is indeed a Holy Land. It is the universal dominion

37

of God.

Mohammed castigated the social injustice prevalent in the rich merchant city of pre-Islamic Mecca. Very rich and very poor people faced each other. The Mecca which Mohammed aimed at was to be a just city. As a Muslim Mohammed did not aim at the redemption of history but at a solution of the historic process. His just city was a utopia come true. Slowly but radically Zionism left the messianic pretensions of Shabbatai Zevi behind and became a national movement with Jerusalem as its Jewish Mecca.

With the Zionist movement Jewish messianism found a new outlet into history. Zionism is different from medieval messianism such as that of Shabbatai Zevi. Yet Zionism too awakened in its followers the feverish passion of former Jewish pilgrims to reach Zion, which had become a new Zion. It was propagated like any utopian movement of the modern age. It had received a new name. The name was: a homeland for Jews. Yet Zionism must not be wholly identified with any of the utopian movements, be they nationalist or socialist. Utopian man is creative man relying only on himself and his ideal. In the Zionist movement the pilgrim journeying to the Holy Land appeared in a modern garb.

The utopian ideal of Zion as a homeland did not make Jews leave the diaspora in great numbers. A force outside Zionism made it different from any utopian movement. In Zionism the terrible but holy force of the election of the Jewish people rose from the depth in which it could have been regarded as asleep for a time. It reappeared and made Jews leave the diaspora. God the Creator brought Israel back to its homeland.

The poem of Judah ha-Levi in which he refers to his long delay in setting out for his pilgrimage to the Holy Land is revealing. He was determined to go. But he postponed his departure from one month to the next, from one year to the next. Then something happened which forced him to go. He does not tell us what made him leave his home in which he was happy and where he was known and honoured as a poet and as a scholar. His poems were sometimes read out in the synagogue which he attended. He did not go as a result of a personal decision, he was forced to go. Messianism is different from utopianism. In messianism it is not human decision which is the driving force moving history. A force outside man transforms him into messianic man. In Zionism the messianically motivated Jew came to the fore and changed history. Jews who loved their home in the diaspora went to Palestine. The Holy Land, a spiritual abode to the medieval Jew, became Israel, a land on the geographer's map.

In Israel the Sabbatian messianism of nineteenth-century Zionism came to an end. The establishment of the State of Israel proved to be a political event of importance. It was not a messianic event. *Galut* continued. Israel was *'galut arab'*, as Dubnow called it. To live in the *galut* remained the fate of the people chosen by God to be the *am ehad*, the peculiar people. Whatever the Zionists may say, a new chapter has started, and it is a chapter in the history of exile. We find ourselves again as the people living under the conditions of the diaspora. Israel itself is within the diaspora. *Galut* does not merely mean 'outside the boundaries of the Holy Land', it means the unredeemed land. Jews must be able and are able to live in this world in which the Messiah has not yet arrived.

The gentile as pagan man is a terrible animal. But as the carrier of developed civilization and culture the gentile world offers the Jew possibilities of creative activity. Stefan Zweig with his 'I love the diaspora' refers to the culture in which Jews can participate in the diaspora. Jewish culture is possible where the Christian division between spiritual and secular has created besides work and prayer a third realm: culture. The Hebrew word *avodah* means both work and worship. Franz Rosenzweig reminds us that in biblical Hebrew we have no word for culture. The biblical Jew knows man as a worker and as a worshipper. Man as the creator of culture is not within the biblical imagination. It is because the gentile Christian has devised a third human function, that of creating culture, in addition to work and worship, that Jewish culture exists. It is not paradoxical but realistic to say that where there is Christian culture, the culture of western man, Jewish culture can flourish. Jewish culture is the gift of the diaspora to the Jewish people.

39

The essays of many nineteenth-century Hebrew writers are often shallow examples of Jewish culture. The creations of Spanish and German Jewry in literature and art show what great height can be reached in Jewish culture. But in no case must Judaism, that is Prophetic Judaism, be identified with Jewish culture, as is done by the non-Jewish Jews of our age. Living in the diaspora, living in constant dialogue with the religions and ideas of the gentiles, Jewish life is prevented from becoming stagnant and sterile nationalism. The skullcap was once used as a Jewish religious headgear. Today it has become a piece of uniform for the Orthodox Jew. Every army has its uniform. The skullcap is today a reminder of how strongly comtemporary Jewry has become politicised.

The Good Life outside the State — the Bourgeois
A price has to be paid by anybody who becomes a citizen of a western State, and it is an urgent task to investigate what kind of price this is. With his citizenship the Jew enters a world in which the dichotomy spiritual-secular unavoidably rises to the surface. This dichotomy is both religious and political. Franz Rosenzweig with his decisive insight that Jews 'do not have to hire the services of the spirit' (*Star*, p. 299) was the first Jew to understand the involvement of the State in Christianity.

The State remains bound up with the dualism: God and Caesar. The citizen is involved in the unremitting obligation to commitments which demand from him 'services of the spirit'. Jewish life remains family life. But this life is split into two spheres when the Jew, when any man for that matter, becomes a citizen. The citizen leaves the compact oneness of reality and faces two forms of reality, the spiritual and the secular. The citizen moves in relentless dialectics either to the cruel secularity which the Roman State displayed and which the modern totalitarian State wishes to revive, or he is on his way to the Christian faith. The Jewish character is shaped without a spiritual influence.

Yet as a citizen the Jew enters and is influenced by the spiritual realm. The Jew is not a Jew through the spirit. He is

40

more — any Jew will say. He is less — any Christian will say. The citizen is made aware of a dual duty, the duty to God and the duty to the Caesar. The State makes the citizen a secular person, but one who has spiritual duties. The citizen is a citizen-soldier, and the soldier's duty, his finest, is to lay down his life on the altar of the fatherland. *Morituri te salutant.* The sacrificial duties of the citizen are demanded by the secular State as they are by the Christian Church. Sacrifice, obedience, loyalty are not merely rendered to the State, to the Caesar, they are enforced by the Caesar. Is he a moloch, or is he the glorious transformer of the citizen into a spiritual figure? Is he a transformer of stones into bread? Is he a transformer of man, of the citizen-soldier, into a superman, a hero, a saint, a god-man? Jew, Christian and Muslim will give their different answers. This is the reason which prevented Rosenzweig from joining the ranks of the Zionists. Admittedly, it is a theological reason. But theological reasons are important. The State can never allow the citizen to forget or to ignore the antithesis Church–State, God–Caesar, spiritual–secular. The Jew is bidden to sanctify life. Sanctification is not spiritualisation. Spiritualisation and sanctification are two different functions. Only the family and communal life, identified with the family, can be sanctified. Political life cannot be sanctified, though it can be spiritualised. The concept 'secular reality' implies a devalued reality. The concept 'profane reality' does not mean a devaluation of reality. To be profane means, in its derivation from the Latin, being 'outside': outside the holy, but on the same level as the holy. The family is neither spiritual nor secular, but it is holy.

The genius of Islam has conceived a type of citizen who stands outside political life. The *dhimmis* of Islamic law are the citizens who do not belong either to the conquerors or to the conquered. They pay a tax and have a place which a westerner would call with dismay that of second-class citizen. But the privilege — and it is a privilege — of belonging to the class of the *dhimmis* is granted only to 'people of Scripture', to Jews, Christians and Sabaeans. Having given its proper due to the western protest we may ask whether all middle classes have not

41

like the *dhimmis* received their magna charta, which allows them to stand outside politics and to live, if not in real freedom, yet under the rule of justice.

The Arabs were surprised when they saw Jews as soldiers. In their view this is not the role assigned to Jews by God. Priests do not wield weapons. Are Zionists still Jews? Surely, they are *dhimmis*, the Muslim argues. According to Muslim theology *dhimmis* have their peaceful professions: they are famous doctors to kings (Maimonides), they are treasurers, promoting the prosperity of the countries in which they live. Jews are scholars who excel in learning. It was thus that the Muslims saw the Jews, when they acknowledged them in their privileged status as *dhimmis*. But the Zionists did not agree with the medieval form of tolerance, which, in any case, the Muslim alone, never the Christian, granted to the Jew. The Zionists made the law of the *polis* their own. The Zionist is a western Jew. He has stepped out of the orbit of Islamic culture, which often made medieval civilization a human place for the Jew. The Zionists have become implicated in the dilemma which the *polis* poses for man.

When the *muezzin* invites all men to worship, he invites to *al-falah*. This Arabic word denotes the good life granted by Allah. In the two thousand years of Christianity no respected place was ever accorded to the bourgeois. It cannot be denied that a stigma of contempt surrounds both bourgeois and *dhimmi*. Christian and Arabic feudal lords are a caste of warriors and hold the peaceful bourgeois and *dhimmi* in disrespect. According to Christian evaluation, the bourgeois is not a saint or a sinner; he is one of those whom Dante saw outside and not inside Paradise. With the western world becoming a bourgeois society Islam, not Christianity, is fit to justify the bourgeois, and at this point the Jew decidedly walks with the Muslim, not with the Christian. All conquerors see a stumbling block in bourgeois human existence, when they call people away from their homes and make them march to the battlefields in pursuit of spiritual aims and values. The aim of the crusader is spiritual. On the way to the Holy Land the crusaders arranged pogroms. In Vienna, when it was still populated with Jews, Jewish children ran away from young hooligans whom they called *pülcher*. In this word the word 'pilgrim' was preserved. The same word for pilgrim and hooligan! Christian society, truly analysed according to Christian dogma, could find no place for the Jew; Muslim society could. The bourgeois of the west and the *dhimmi* in the midst of Islam find their happiness by standing outside the State. But happiness it is, as long as it lasts. The communist poet Bertold Brecht is still a Christian when he writes about the 'deadly sins' of the bourgeois.

Art and science are enriched by the sons of bourgeois parents. Bourgeois society, although radically different from the State, provides the State with a creative type of man. The State itself is in its nucleus always a Spartan State, politically effective but culturally sterile. The State is — as Ortega y Gasset calls it — an 'empty space', where people do not have homes. The 'empty space' is the place where the orators argue their reasons to the populace and issue their marching orders, but it itself is nothing. The discovery of this empty space in the *polis*, the understanding of the *forum*, alone explains the essence of the State. The 'empty space' within the State sucks away all creative strength from the human unit which surrounds it. In the ambivalence of the State as a nothing and at the same time as a centre, western man's political life is mapped out. The State robs its children of their freedom to live in bourgeois happiness, but gives them the freedom to be independent of tribal life and of the ruthless chance prevalent in nature. The State establishes law. This law, the law of the State, the political law, is the beginning and the end of the freedom of man. This law liberates us from the jungle, but binds us to the force of political inevitability. In the way in which this law is interpreted, accepted and rejected, Jew, Christian and Muslim go different ways.

Nowadays people speak in a most unthinking way of Jewish law. There are, of course, ordinances, precepts and, above all, there is the moral law, which can be summarised in the notion of a Jewish law. But it must be clear that the law of the *polis* is not to be identifield with a law which can rightly be called Jewish law. The law of the *polis* transports man into the world of tragic heroism. It makes man aspire to the glory of Greek

43

antiquity. The law of the city makes man political man, makes him leave father and mother and directs him towards the place where man kills man, yet is not a murderer, but Cain, invested with the glory of a hero. The law which is truly Jewish law establishes peace and brotherhood.

Humanisation is the Jewish, spiritualisation the Christian, submission the Islamic attitude towards the State. The Jew as citizen endeavours to remain 'the merciful offspring of merciful forebears'. The Christian will transform the tragedy of political life by aiming eventually to make the State a Church. The Muslim submits in unquestioning obedience to the State, which he regards as a religious institution. He does not expect nor does he demand freedom from the State, which he sees as the guarantor of justice. Denied the possession of freedom, the Muslim is not western man.

The Arabic dictionary explains the word *al-falah* as welfare and good life. The call of the *muezzin* from the minaret invites man to a life which we could identify with bourgeois happiness. But to the possible meanings of *al-falah* one important one has still to be added: paradise. The *muezzin* invites man not only to join the people rejoicing in the good life, he also invites him to enter the non-terrestrial glory of the world to come. In the case of the Muslim we cannot speak of a spiritual realm, we must speak of a non-terrestrial realm. *Al-falah* does not merely denote earthly good life, it points to the transcendent world, as do all three monotheistic religions.

The sociologist who treats the bourgeois as a social or as a political type is well advised to learn from the Arabic dictionary that *al-falah* includes references to the world of transcendence. It is futile to hope to get an understanding of the bourgeois through a merely sociological approach. A theological analysis alone can succeed in explaining the depth of bourgeois life. Bourgeois life interrupts political life as an oasis breaks up the scenery of the desert. The way of political man, alas, is often a way through a desert. The chapters of history in which bourgeois life prevails bring blessing. The biblical prophets urge the people never to give up hope. When the tempest of political confrontation is over, blessing will be the happy por-

44

tion of man. Indeed, a large part of the prophetic message identifies blessing with bourgeois happiness. The messianic expectation of the prophets waits for the day when the apocalyptic horsemen threatening the homes of man with hunger and war have gone.

None of the three monotheistic religions can be excluded when bourgeois social life is under consideration. The Islamic scholar Karl Becker called Islam a 'carrier of religion'. It can be said of any bourgeoisie that it is a carrier of religion. Nowadays we often find Judaism identified with bourgeois life. The Jew has been called the typical bourgeois. But we can also at times be justified in speaking of a Christian or an Islamic bourgeoisie. Bourgeois groups are in themselves religiously neutral, but in this neutrality they are most fit to be called 'carriers of religion', carriers of Judaism or of Christianity or of Islam.

Having said this we must admit that a Jewish bourgeoisie is more apt to be a carrier of Judaism than a Christian bourgeoisie is able to be a carrier of Christianity. The reason lies in the political element which still prevails within Christianity. A Jewish bourgeoisie, on the other hand, is entirely devoid of a political element in its structure. The Jewish bourgeois can be a Jew in the full sense of the word, whereas the Christian bourgeois has not retained the full power of his Christian spirituality. The Christian as a bourgeois remains a *zoon politikon*, a political social type. He is not in a position in which he can ignore his political commitments. He decidedly obeys Caesar, or at least Caesar more than God.

What makes the Jewish bourgeois a religious figure far beyond ambiguity and neutrality is the Jewish attitude to power, to force, to violence. Jew and bourgeois walk through history like priests. The priest does not wield a sword. No ideology lures the bourgeois into battle. The bourgeois remains a bourgeois as long as he is a private person. The words of Gideon 'I will not rule over you, nor shall my son; the Lord will rule over you' (Judges 8, 23) makes the Kingdom of God the only social order of which the bourgeois can approve. Peace is the only social condition under which the bourgeois can flourish. There is no political system which can truly and lastingly

45

provide mankind with peace. Peace is the fruit growing in the Kingdom of God. The Kingdom of God not as an ideology, but as the home in which man can live on this earth, exists when a bourgeoisie is existentially established. The *muezzin* inviting man to a life outside the State, to *al-falah*, to terrestrial welfare, sees the kingdom of Allah granted to man in the peace of bourgeois life. Who is a bourgeois? The Jew? The Christian? The Muslim? Anyone whose political 'ideology' can truly be expressed in the word peace. The words *shalom, salam, pax* bring the holy message of God to man. The bourgeois is Abel, who enjoys God's favour: in his contented husbandry he is radically different from Cain.

Man as Citizen.
In memory of the Israeli Soldiers who fell in the
Yom Kippur War
Throughout my theological writings I have had to emphasize that the Christian is not born a Christian but that he becomes a Christian. The Jew, on the other hand, is born a Jew. The situation of the citizen is similar to that of the Christian. The citizen becomes a citizen. Nobody is born a citizen.

Franz Rosenzweig stresses the fact that the only characteristic of the Jew is his being man. His common bond with his fellow Jew and with his fellow man is the blood which is the same in every man's veins. It is therefore a misunderstanding to see Rosenzweig as a racist. At the time when he wrote, racism was not yet the widely discussed problem which it became later. Rosenzweig uses the word blood in the sense of the biblical 'flesh and blood'. Blood, seen by Rosenzweig as the constituent of life, points to the family bond between man and man and between Jew and Jew. Blood, not ideology, is the decisive factor. Blood, not spiritual succession, guarantees lasting history. Blood and not cerebral examination and planning brings us face to face with reality. He rejects the ideologies which politicised Judaism offers in union with Liberalism or Nationalism or Socialism. Rosenzweig's trust in reality leads him 'into life'. 'Life' and 'blood' are the keywords of Rosenzweig's religious realism. He meets God in the reality of life. He has no need 'to hire the services of the spirit' (*Star*, p. 299) to meet God. He explains his religious realism in a letter to his mother: 'What matters is to have one's five senses open to the world, so open that even *der liebe Gott* may appear as present in it' (*Trialogue*, p. 80).

The humanity of the Jew is his only decisive characteristic. Our understanding of what the Jew is turns to the family and not to the State. The Jew is a Jew in the family. In the State man is a citizen. The citizen is a citizen not merely through 'the blood'. He is a citizen through the impact of the historic forces which make him a secular type. Man can only become secular man through his previous participation in the spiritual realm. The Christian understands the Church as a spiritual body. Her secularisation gave birth to State and citizen. It was a mistake of the Jewish Enlightenment Movement to see the Jewish citizen as a man like any other man, the difference being 'only' in his faith. All citizens are the same kind of persons. They differ only in their faith, in the religious denomination. The Christian citizen was regarded as the same social type as the Jewish citizen. Both were citizens. Citizenship was thought to do away with the civic disabilities of the Jew. This new situation was rightly hailed as the great gift which Emancipation presented to the Jew. So far so good. But what about the price which the Jew had to pay? As a citizen the Jew was no longer a man like any man, he became, like the Christian, a 'changed man'. The politicisation of the Jew set in and changed him into a secular person. The process of secularisation gave birth to the citizen of the western world.

The ideologists of the Jewish Enlightenment Movement coined the formula 'German (or French or British or American or whatever the case may be) citizen of the Jewish faith'. It was overlooked that the Jew as citizen was no longer merely what every man is: a creature in whom the 'blood', identical in every man, is the only characteristic. It was overlooked that the Jewish citizen was a changed man, changed by his participation in a history which had secularised the Church. The Jewish citizen was not — and is not — merely man, but secular man.

47

The Jewish citizen is — or at least can become — secular man; the Jewish citizen can become a Jewish gentile. The word gentile must retain its biblical meaning: the gentiles possess the nobility of being indigenous people. A gentile is not an immigrant. Could not citizenship change a Jew into a kind of Jewish gentile? What can be suggested about the Jewish gentile of the Enlightenment era can also be said of the Jews of the Zionist era. We have become acquainted with the Israeli gentile. We have also spoken of the non-Jewish Jew and have called him a politicised, i.e. a secularised Jew. But only what was first spiritual can become secular. Our modern politicised Judaism is the consequence of our entry into the western world, which is a Christian world, a secularised Christian world but a Christian world just the same. The diaspora Jew as a patriotic citizen and the Zionist are the outcome of a history moving close to Christianity.

Jews approached the dilemma 'God or Caesar' and were forced to solve it both in the diaspora and in the Holy Land. The historians record the heroism of the citizen-soldier. Since the establishment of the State the Israeli citizen-soldiers have fought and died in three wars, like the Greek soldiers at Thermopylae, whose tomb bore the words:

Stranger, go tell the Lacedaemonians
that we lie here
obedient to their commands.

Heroism is noble. But the Yom Kippur War demands more than a monument for heroism. We are living in cataclysmic times. We are confronted with a history which displays its power of mighty transformation. We must ask ourselves, what does God want from us at this juncture of history? God calls to all fathers: 'Do not raise your hand against the boy; do not touch him' (Genesis 22, 8). There is *kiddush hashem* (the sanctification of the name of God), and there is *jihad* (holy war). Every national war is *jihad*. *Kiddush hashem* — unlike *jihad* — forfeits any creative ambition which is so strong in the fighters of *jihad*.

We shall remember the Israelis who died in the Yom Kippur War, as we remember our kith and kin who have passed away.

We remember them in the Memorial Services of our Jewish Year. *Mazkir neshamot,* Remembrance of the Souls of the Departed, not hero worship, is our attitude.

The tragedy of the dying soldier is noble tragedy. But of holy tragedy we Jews do not speak. In the centre of the Christian faith the pious Christian is consoled and guided by the memorial of a holy tragedy: the suffering Servant dying in pain and agony on the cross. The Israeli soldier died to save the State, to rescue his kith and kin from agony, murder and rape. We are entitled to see the death of the Israeli citizen soldier as *kiddush hashem*, as the sanctification of the name of God. True, in this *kiddush hashem*, for which the young Israelis died, is involved what is not holy. We need not, we must not, forget the wrong generalship, the misguided politics and the clinging to an out-dated ideology, of which the war dead were victims. It is therefore appropriate for us to say: they died *mipnei hataeinu*, because of our sins.

After an interval of centuries — from the year 70 up to 1948 — the Jewish people is again in charge of a State. In the diaspora and in his Jewish State the Jew has become western man, by whom statehood is highly valued. Yet, as a politicised Jew he is not always and not in every respect what the prophets and the classical rabbis desired the Jew to be. The difference between the Jewish people and the gentiles has in a new and grave form become the problem of contemporary Jewry.

It is sixty years since Franz Rosenzweig wrote his *Star of Redemption*. A cogent passage is quoted here in conclusion of this essay. In it Rosenzweig rejected the idea that a state should be the *summum bonum* for Jewish belief. Today our generation defends the State of Israel with the heroism of the citizen-soldier who died at Thermopylae. Surely, the least we can say is that Rosenzweig's view is not applicable to our present situation. But we must say more. We can only reject Rosenzweig in the way in which the kings of Israel and Judah rejected the political guidance of the prophets. The kings saw the advice of the prophets as not applicable to any political situation. The prophetic demands were rejected. And yet these rejected prophets were not unsuccessful. They made the Jewish people a

49

nation different from the gentiles. We must heed Rosenzweig's
words, even if we reject them as unsuitable for practical political life. Rosenzweig's negative attitude towards the State is the
attitude of the prophets. The State, alas, demands and receives
the sacrifice of the citizen-soldiers, who shed their blood to
defend it. The prophetic pronouncement of Rosenzweig reads:

> The peoples of the world are not content with the
> bonds of blood. They sink their roots into the night
> of earth, lifeless in itself but the spender of life, and
> from the lastingness of earth they conclude that they
> themselves will last. Their will to eternity clings to
> the soil and to the reign over the soil, to the land. The
> earth of their homeland is watered by the blood of
> their sons, for they do not trust in the life of a
> community of blood, in a community that can dis-
> pense with anchorage in solid earth. We were the
> only ones who trusted in blood and abandoned the
> land; and so we preserved the priceless sap of life
> which pledged us that it would be eternal. Among
> the peoples of the world, we were the only ones who
> separated what lived within us from all community
> with what is dead. For while the earth nourishes, it
> also binds. Whenever a people loves the soil of its
> native land more than its own life, it is in danger — as
> all the people of the world are — that, though nine
> times out of ten this love will save the native soil from
> the foe and, along with it, the life of the people, in the
> end the soil will persist as that which was loved more
> strongly, and the people will leave their lifeblood
> upon it. In the final analysis, the people belong to
> him who conquers the land. It cannot be otherwise,
> because people cling to the soil more than to their life
> as a people. Thus the earth betrays a people that
> entrusted its permanence to earth. The soil endures,
> the peoples who live on it pass.

(pp. 299–300)

The State and the Rise of Christianity

For the man of Greek antiquity State and Church were identical. The Christian Church had not yet made its appearance on the stage of history, but the Greek citizen looked upon the *polis* as being both State and Church. The pagan Greek State was revered in the way the gods were revered. The *polites*, the citizen, defended his city in the hour of war with the same devotion with which Christians would make their sacrifices for their spiritual cause. The State was surrounded by a numinous aura. The citizen was a soldier. He could also be an artist. The Greek city, any city of antiquity, was populated with gods, and the citizen as artist was busily occupied creating the marble wonders of the gods of the city.

The citizen as artist went through a change which transformed man, the creature of God, into man, the creator. This change elevated the artist into a higher sphere. In this elevation man leaves the secular and enters the spiritual sphere. The rise of Christianity also begins with man transfigured through pain and toil into another being: into a being with spiritual propensities. The life of the artist is like the life of a saint; it is a story of a constant sacrifice. Christianity is the story of a sacrifice. A Jew may cry out: 'My God, my God, why hast Thou forsaken me?' A Christian submits to God who does not send the message: 'Lay not thy hand upon the lad, neither do thou any thing unto him' (Genesis 22, 12). In the faith of the Christian the sacrifice is needed as a means to the elevation into the spiritual realm, for the transfiguration of the secular into the spiritual.

Not only the artist but any soldier who fights and dies is led to the tragic hour when man changes his status of creature of God into man the creator. There God accepts, as the Christian story goes, the sacrifices which make a battlefield a place where men die in terrible agony. The cross is an instrument of torture and sadistically inflicted pain. The Romans invented it and used it throughout the whole era of their dictatorial reign. The crosses around Jerusalem and a tank battle imprisoning soldiers in burning tanks hardly find an equivalent in the sadistic imagination which conjures up hell. The fear of hell always haunted medieval man. And yet the Cross has become the symbol of

51

Christianity. It lifts the Christian praying to God to spiritual height. The transfiguration of secular man into spiritual man is the content of the Christian faith. Political man is secular man. We cannot understand Christianity without understanding the State. The Church is a spiritualised State. The rise of Christianity happens through a sacrifice suffered and not avoided. What the Gospels tell us about Christ is the story of a man entirely human and at the same time a spiritual being. Christianity answers the challenge with which tragedy confronts a human life. Surely God, the omnipotent God, has the power to save man from the bitter implication of tragedy. It says in the Old Testament: 'And God saw all He had made, and it was very good' (Genesis 1, 31). What about Job? The Jew has one answer: 'Behold, I am of small account. . . I lay my hand upon my mouth' (Job 40, 4). The Jew bypasses tragedy. He does not solve the riddle of tragedy in a good world. The Christian solves the riddle. The man suffering and dying on the Cross becomes the symbol of an elevation to a sphere in which no tragedy exists, no tears are shed, no pain is endured. The Christian kneels before the Cross and worships God who transports man from the here and now to the spiritual realm. 'The dying Gaul' is a sculpture by a Greek artist which he has succeeded in imbuing with beautified features. Dying of his wounds the soldier looks up to God who will be with him after death. He and the Man on the Cross have one message: 'the fifth act of the tragedy is victory, *though* a spiritual victory', says the Jew. But the Christian says: 'A spiritual victory is a true victory'. Jew and Christian are near to each other in the message they bring to man. Still, they are apart from each other, because the word spiritual is not to be found in the holy books of the Jew.

Franz Rosenzweig realised that Herzl's *Judenstaat* was a liberal State which does not face the tragedy implicit in political life. The State is the beginning of human freedom. It transforms a jungle into a rationally ordered society. But the State can also be the end of human freedom, because it coerces man. Political rule enforces its laws through power. The Cross is the symbol of power, of Roman power. Power rules cruelly.

Rosenzweig explained to his Zionist friends why he could not reconcile Jewish existence with the ambition of aspiring to a Jewish State: it is the Christian mission to convert the State. It is the Christian mission to transform the Cross, the instrument of cruel torture and murder, into a symbol of charity, kindness and peace. It is the Christian mission to spiritualise the State into a Church. The Jew sees the good life outside the State. The Cross is there in the midst of the State. Long before the Constantinian State-Church relationship was established, the political and the spiritual element in Christianity existed side by side, there was a political and a spiritual message of the Christian Church. The Christian obeys God *and* Caesar. The slogan should not merely read: God *or* Caesar. To Franz Rosenzweig it was evident that Jews in charge of a Jewish State would have to become 'Christians'. Only Christians are called to transform and are capable of transfiguring the 'beast' into the 'Lamb of God'.

As an historical document the New Testament is a most unreliable source. Great Christians like Pascal, Kierkegaard or Dostoevski searched their own heart rather than the pages of the New Testament when they desired their conversion to the Christian faith. The New Testament sometimes has a gnostic, a Hellenistic message. It changes Pilate, that cruel Machiavellian, into a benevolent liberal-minded gentleman. All this has been made clear through the masterly exegesis of the New Testament of H. Maccoby, Paul Winter, S.G.F. Brandon and R. Bultmann. These scholars show the antagonism between Christianity with its roots in a political situation and Judaism with its roots in the family. Christianity spiritualises the State into a Church, Judaism sanctifies the family and upholds the peace and kindness of family life for all the patterns of social life. The rise of Christianity out of a political pre-history is overlooked by people who speak today of the State merely as 'government'. This one-sided view makes the State an economic institution like a huge limited company. Rosenzweig goes to the roots. He asks in epistemological caution: 'What is the *polis* after all?'

Judaism and Christianity are two ways to God, with Islam as a third way. But Islam is not really a third way. It is a way to God as a 'carrier' of Judaism and Christianity. The difference between the two ways can sometimes, alas often, amount to a confrontation, and then we are entitled to speak of 'Christian antisemitism'. But the new era of demythologisation enables Judaism and Christianity to see each other as monotheistic religions. After all, the 'tree', Christianity, destined to cover the whole world, grows from the 'seed' which is Judaism. The two ways to God, Judaism and Christianity, remain different, but as Franz Rosenzweig does not tire of emphasizing, 'God needs them both'.

IV

Home and History

Compassion for Jezebel

EVERY Jewish and Christian child who attends religion classes knows Jezebel as the wicked queen who deserved her end, described in cruel detail in 2 Kings (9, 33). Yet Jezebel was a religious woman, although her religion was not that of the prophet Elijah, who preached his fierce sermons which condemned Jezebel and her husband Ahab, the king of Israel. Ahab was the last king of the Northern Kingdom who, through wise diplomacy and through contracts with the great powers, could have saved Israel. He was obstructed and eventually defeated by the wild prophet Elijah. Elijah can be called the Mohammed of the Old Testament. He raged against Ahab's attempt to establish a progressive synthesis of prophetic desert tradition and Canaanite agricultural civilization. The latter had developed in and around the cities of Israel and Judah. Centuries later Mohammed's armies fought against the Hellenistic Christian urban communities. Elijah too was hostile to a civilization and a religion which, in the villages and in the cities, worshipped God not in the way of the fathers but in the happy mood of the recipients of 'corn, new wine and oil' (Hosea 2, 8). There was no use in Hosea's reminding the people that God himself was the giver of 'corn, new wine and oil'. To Elijah this God was — baal. City-civilization, it was argued, made man forsake God. To live in houses instead of in tents meant to 'go a-whoring after the baal'. Eventually it was not Elijah but Hosea and prophets like him who forged the controversy between monotheism outside history and within it into a monotheism which worshipped God both in and outside the home, both in the family and in the market place, both in private life and in public. The Rehabites who insisted on living only in tents did

55

not have the last word. They disappeared from Jewish history. The prophets who insisted that both the tent in the desert and the house in the city are the place where God can be worshipped eventually dominated Jewish life.

The Still, Small Voice

God is to be found in the withdrawn patriarchal togetherness and also in history. The meaning of the words 'the still, small voice' (I Kings 19, 12) rejects Elijah's ecstasy and his political zealotry which makes him prone to appear more like a Muslim than like a biblical prophet. Judging the patriarchs and the prophets the Koran has its own opinion regarding their importance or unimportance. Mohammed approves of the patriarchs: they become Koranic figures. With the prophets it is different. The great prophets of the Bible from the eighth century onward are entirely absent in the Koran. The sequence stops with Elijah. Amos, Hosea, the Isaiahs, Jeremiah are not mentioned by Mohammed. He ignores them, because he opposes them. The Islamic opposition makes them Christian figures. The Jew faces therefore a significant dilemma. Refusing to see the biblical prophets interpreted as Christian figures he moves towards an Islamic interpretation of the prophets. Refusing to see them in the way of Islamic interpretation he moves towards a Christian interpretation. We arrive here at a point where we have to elucidate Jewish monotheism in its relationship to Christianity and Islam. Not only the Jewish theologian but every Jew who reads or hears the prophetic lesson in synagogue must make a decision: should he understand the prophetic texts in the Islamic or in the Christian way? Is Elijah a Jewish Mohammed? Are Isaiah, Hosea, Jeremiah to be seen in the way in which the theologians of the Christian Church see them?

A New Interpretation of an Old Metaphor

Judah ha-Levi and Maimonides see Judaism as the seed which brings forth the tree with the two branches: Christianity and Islam. They dare to see Judaism, Christianity and Islam, in

56

spite of their differences, as identical in so far as they are forms of monotheism. But it is an entirely new interpretation, not envisaged either by Judah ha-Levi or by Maimonides, when we say that there is Christianity and Islam within Judaism, that Christianity and Islam are already there within the 'seed' itself and not merely later in the tree with the two branches. Anybody who accepts the metaphor of the seed and the tree in this new way has left the Middle Ages. Judah ha-Levi and Maimonides did not leave the Middle Ages, even if they admitted the equal status of the three monotheistic religions. They did not discover the possibility of seeing Christianity and Islam within Judaism. This entirely novel insight glares into the face of modern man, be he Jew, Christian or Muslim.

Yet the metaphor of the seed and the tree can, indeed must, be understood by the post-medieval Jew as meaning that Christianity and Islam are within Judaism. To call Elijah the Mohammed of the Old Testament is only one example to which we are able to add many others showing an Islamic or Christian doctrine or form of behaviour within Judaism, within the Jewish Scriptures. It is not enough to talk of a dialogue between Jew, Christian and Muslim. Such a dialogue is valuable and takes place now wherever peace and reconciliation between Jew, Christian and Muslim are pursued. A dialogue can take place between people who are different from each other. In pointing to Christianity and Islam within Judaism we realise that Judaism, Christianity and Islam are often not different from each other. With this understanding the dialogue ceases to be an intellectual enterprise and becomes a meeting similar to a meeting of kinsmen. Brothers meet brothers.

This absolutely novel perspective makes our age as revolutionary as the age which followed the year 70 C.E., the year of the destruction of the Temple. 'How shall we remain Jews without the Temple?' asked the Jews of that cataclysmic era. 'How shall we remain Jews?' asks the present generation, 'without the shelter of that separate identity which makes us different from Christians and Muslims? Are we not deprived of that shelter when it is said that there is Christianity and Islam within Judaism?'

57

Far from being weakened, the knowledge of our difference from the other two monotheistic religions has been strengthened by three facts. Firstly, the recognition of Christianity and Islam within Judaism shows the Jewish people as giving birth to Christianity and Islam. Secondly, historical criticism and demythologisation have made Jewish history and Jewish principles truly visible and put an end to the falsifying approach of medieval apologists. Thirdly, there is the State of Israel as preserver of the separate role of Judaism at the side of Christianity and Islam. With the establishment of the State of Israel 'the fence around the Torah' is no longer needed for the protection of individual Jewish identity.

Asia, with its religious nihilism and its mysticism, threatens the west and makes Judaism indispensable and therefore more distinguishable. By acknowledging Christianity and Islam within Judaism we acknowledge ourselves generally as monotheists and not merely as an individual religion of monotheism. Jews, Christians and Muslims — we are all monotheists. As a united monotheistic civilization, poised against Hinduism and Buddhism, we critically watch the individual contribution of each of the three monotheistic religions. In one case Judaism, in another Christianity or Islam will become our defence against the threat of what is neither Judaism nor Christianity nor Islam. All three monotheistic religions are different and all three are needed when we guard the border against the invasion of modern barbarism. Jew, Christian and Muslim have each a different mission to perform in history. This different mission created their different identity and preserves it within their common identity as monotheistic faith.

Not Spiritual, yet Holy

Jew, Christian and Muslim must necessarily remain different from each other. The world of the Christian is constituted by using the categories spiritual and secular. The world of the Jew is constituted using the categories holy and profane. The Jew does not need to step towards a spiritual sphere in order to meet God. The Jew knows what the word holy denotes. He has been told: 'Ye shall be holy, because I, the Lord, am holy'. The Jew has been told, nobody is holy but God. The Jew knows very well what the word spiritual denotes. But whereas the Christian enters the realm of the spiritual by entering the Christian Church, the Jew does not need the atmosphere of the spiritual when praying to God. Yet modern Jews know — and cherish — the spiritual world of art, of western culture. The Jew, like any Christian, is uplifted by listening to great music, by reading poems, in short, by meeting the artist and admiring his work. Here, Jew and Christian will not agree with each other; it is already much that they understand each other's different approach. The Christian most emphatically rejects the Jew's view that spirit is always the spirit of man. It is already a step forward, a step away from the Middle Ages, that the Jew understands the Christian's objection to identifying spirit with the spirit of man. It is already a step forward that the Christian understands the refusal of the Jew to transform his Judaism into a spiritual Judaism. Yet there it is: a spiritual Judaism exists. The Church is spiritual Judaism. A Judaism without participation in history becomes spiritual Judaism. Cooperation of the diaspora with Jewry in the State of Israel is therefore a Jewish religious duty. It prevents Judaism from becoming spiritual Judaism. Thus it will remain: Jew and Christian, so near to each other, so much dependent on each other for a mission common to both of them are, and indeed must remain, different from each other.

The Jew does not do what the Muslim does. The Muslim rejects spirituality in the realm of culture, he is afraid to be led into apostasy by spirituality, in fact, he dislikes spirituality: the sweet sound of the church bells disgusts him, still reminds him of the pigs which the crusaders herded in mosques. The Jew is without the Muslim's antipathy. He likes, loves, approves of spirituality which he finds in the culture of western man and to which he makes his valuable contribution. Of course, the 'Jewish culture' of the western Jew is an offshoot of Christian culture.

Jewish intellectuals were able to render an important contribution to western culture. It is their 'Christianity' within their Judaism which enabled them to do so. But all avenues of culture have been trodden and the *fin de siècle* spirit begins to make itself felt. Is the end of culture *ennui*? Some say so. But a way out is possible, and is given to our generation through the example of Franz Rosenzweig. At the height of the culture of his time he turned away from the belief in a solution through culture, through art, philosophy and literature. He turned to the biblical world. He learned Hebrew and read the Bible — as he had previously read Goethe.

Jewish novelists in America delve deep into the important content of twentieth-century culture. If they emulate the conversion of Franz Rosenzweig — not a 'Damascus', but a conversion just the same — they, these gifted writers Isaac Bashevis Singer, Bernard Malamud, Saul Bellow, have much to give to our embattled age. But what these Jews have to undergo is the conversion from literature to theology. They have to do what Rosenzweig did.

The Family

Secularisation has made all three monotheistic religions leave their ghettos. The Christian Church — that splendid Christian ghetto of the Middle Ages — is today like Judaism and Islam a denomination furthering its religious aims. This does not mean that secularisation has made the three monotheistic religions disappear from civilization. They are present in a new form. Western man of the secular age is still a Jew or a Christian or a Muslim. Whether or not he confesses his loyalty to one of the three religions, he remains a Jew, a Christian, a Muslim. The walls of the ghettos have disappeared and this makes monotheism even stronger than it was in the Middle Ages. Shakespeare is a typical man of the Renaissance, but in his *Sonnets* or in his *Tempest* he is a most articulate Christian. Secularisation does not obliterate any of the three monotheistic religions. The danger which secularisation carries in itself is in the political field. Secularisation, particularly that of the Christian Church, brings the naked State, the dreaded Leviathan, to the fore. A secular State, a State not restrained by any form of monotheism, leads to fascism.

The bourgeois, also a product of secularisation, is a most important carrier of monotheism. In our secular age a Church-going Christian, a practising Jew, a pious Muslim need not in truth be adherents of that form of monotheism which they affirm. The three monotheistic religions are now like sparks which are around us and influence, say, a Christian with Jewish ideas or a Jew or a Muslim with Christian ideas. This seeming disorder has its reason in the strength of monotheism in the secular age. It is not at all a sign of weakness. It is not monotheism but theology that is weak in our secular age. We have to acquire a theological training to see the numerous instances in which the three monotheistic religions penetrate each other.

The bourgeois may seem to be far away from Islam, but his devotion to law and his exclusion of love at the side of law make up a man who is essentially a Muslim. It is the philosopher Ortega y Gasset who in two books, *On Love* and *The Revolt of the Masses*, has taught us to see that the bourgeois and the Muslim have something to do with each other. 'It is difficult for the bourgeois and the Muslim . . . to fall in love in an authentic manner. For them life consists in an insistence on what is known and habitual, an unshakable satisfaction with the same daily routine.' (*On Love*, p. 150). Ortega y Gasset, like Franz Rosenzweig a pupil of the Marburg philosopher Hermann Cohen, recognised the bourgeois as the conservative element in western civilization. Instead of using the word bourgeois as a word of abuse — as our left-wing youth does — we must see the bourgeois as a religious figure. This he is according to the Islamic, but not the Christian, values of our secular age. Whatever the economic foundation of a society may be, it is a society enjoying the good life if the bourgeoisie can prosper in it. The working population of the west has opted to be a bourgeoisie. Our western civilization is often (especially in America) called Jewish-Christian civilization. The bourgeois reminds us that it is a Jewish-Christian-Islamic civilization.

There is the poetic image of the wolf and the lamb lying together in peace. A bourgeois society has this fulfilled peace as its goal. Without engagement in war and without the political manipulation of power the bourgeois is different from creative man; he is, on the contrary, the product of creative forces shaping him. He is, above all, the product of the creator who is the Creator of the world and of all men. The bourgeois is more of a creature than the intellectual, the politician, the artist. In the bourgeois we therefore meet man as God created him. The family is economically a bourgeois social group. In this Karl Marx and Friedrich Engels are right. But when Engels ironically speaks of 'the holy family' the pietism of his upbringing is still there in his philosophy of materialism. Priest, prophet, intellectual and artist, the genius and the simple eternal man, whom we see in Adam, each of these varieties of human beings is the offspring of a bourgeois family. Civilizations do not 'decline and fall' with the bourgeois in their midst.

Man grows to full humanity by experiencing the guidance, security and love which only a father and a mother can provide. Everything is said about the bourgeois family and every praise of the bourgeois family is expressed when we can say about it: 'a father is there, a mother is there'. This makes the bourgeois family the holy family of the secular age. Secularisation destroys the myth but, therefore, makes truly visible what is holy.

Amos versus Ibn Khaldun
Long before Edward Gibbon (1739-1794) Ibn Khaldun, a noble, learned and pious Muslim, pondered in the fourteenth century over the problem of the decline and fall of civilizations. Is this process towards the fall of civilizations inevitable? Ibn Khaldun speaks of *asabiyya*. It is translated by some scholars as cohesion. The tribes in the desert represent people outside history. Outside history *asabiyya* works. What happens to *asabiyya* within history? The gift of *asabiyya* makes a people a closed unit. As long as *asabiyya* is there within civilization, civilization is safe and will last. *Asabiyya* does not mean equality. Chieftan and tribesman are bound together as an intimate unit. But they are not equals.

To explain what Ibn Khaldun means by *asabiyya*, I do not explain the anthropological material of the past but refer to my own time. I can understand my own time and shall not become a victim of imaginary primitive societies of the past, constructed through the abstraction of the anthropologist. *Homo sapiens* is there in history, and no preceding history can explain his miraculous appearance. A miracle cannot be explained. *Homo sapiens* is there in history and no theory of evolution leading to him has convincing credibility.

I have understood the romantic concept of *asabiyya* from the tales of Eastern European Jewish immigrants who succeeded in moving from the East End of London to the middle-class affluence of Golders Green. They spoke with nostalgia of their days in the East End. They were poor then, and life was hard, but they remembered what seemed to them a blissful time. 'On Friday evening we closed the shop, a white tablecloth was spread over the counter, two sabbath candles were placed on it. Children and grandchildren or relatives and friends came. The squalor of the East End was forgotten. A gathering of contented people was a united family.' *Asabiyya* in their midst made them dwell outside the predicament of history. Romantic novels about the Jewish past abound.

Great empires, mighty civilizations fall and fade away through the disappearance of *asabiyya*, says Ibn Khaldun. He amplifies this statement by adding that the fall of civilizations is caused by luxury. The biblical prophet diagnoses differently: the civilizations crumble and fade away through injustice. The Christian diagnosis is the most radical: everything and everybody carries the sickness of death in its still blooming life, only the spirit is eternal. Christianity overcomes the painful problem with which the cycle of the rise and fall of civilizations saddens the heart of man by preaching that every civilization will die one day. The Church herself preserves in her own frame a past civilization: the Roman Empire. The way from rise towards fall is a pilgrimage which leads away from the secular to the spiritual sphere. This spells hope and this hope is expressed in the Christian distinction between secular and spiritual: nobody dies, nothing gets lost, the spirit is eternal. The Christian doctrine has grown from the seed of Judaism. Not the Jew, but the Muslim rejects this doctrine.

63

The Muslim adheres to the belief in terrestrial holiness and reveres holy places. The crumbling stones of past civilizations remain dear to the Muslim. The Jew, praying at the Western Wall, follows the Muslim example.

Is Ibn Khaldun, paralysed by the inevitable doom of every civilization, an Islamic Amos? Amos has often been called a 'prophet of doom'. This is wrong. As a Muslim Ibn Khaldun has no other approach to civilization than to see it as material for conquest, in which Allah prevails. 'The sword cleaneth' is a Muslim saying. Truth and justice call for *jihad*, a holy war. The Muslim feature of Amos is not the whole Amos. How sweet, how forgiving, how 'Christian'—or for that matter how Jewish — is his sigh: '. . . it may be that the Lord the God of Hosts will be gracious to the survivors of Joseph' (5, 15). To Ibn Khaldun the fall of a civilization, when the creative strength of *asabiyya* is exhausted, is inevitable as in a Greek tragedy: no man and no God can interfere and stop the oncoming disaster. Not so Amos. He has hope to offer: 'Seek good and not evil, that you may live. . .' (5, 14).

Even the 'gloomy' Amos looks hopefully for survival. The crushed civilization can be revived and live again. 'I will restore the fortunes of my people Israel; they shall rebuild deserted cities and live in them, they shall plant vineyards and drink their wine, make gardens and eat the fruit' '. . . and every hill shall wave with corn.' (9, 14, 13). In each book of our biblical prophets there is a happy end. Ibn Khaldun never records a happy end. After the fall of a civilization he sees only one thing: the sand of the desert covers the palaces and the mosques.

As a biblical prophet Amos must be seen in the same way as Hosea. Hosea, like all the prophets, is aware of the affluence and pleasantness which civilization offers to man and does not comdemn them. The prophets acknowledge 'food and drink, wool and flax, oil and perfumes' (Hosea 2, 5) as God's gift to man. The step into history from dwelling in the home outside history is regarded by the prophets as progress. Luxury may make civilization weak: progress does not. Progress is the very function of history. But the Muslim hails tradition, not progress.

Tradition is the very programme of political romanticism. By clinging to *sunna* (the path trodden before) the Muslim expresses his romanticism. But tradition is not able to halt the fall of a civilization or of a religious institution. History is always history on the move forward. It can move towards the rise of a new creative period or towards the end of such a period. It is not tradition, but the moral fibre of a civilization that offers hope. Moral obedience, law and order preserve the city. The sack of Rome was the destruction for which the decadent leaders in the city were responsible. When the distinction between what is morally good and what is morally wrong is discarded, the barbarians find easy access to the dwellings of civilized man. Do not blame God for the fall of Jerusalem, said the prophets, blame yourselves. Both the rise and the fall of civilizations are human handiwork. The barbarians had dwelt a long time in a city before they hurled their cruel columns against it.

We have still to take cognizance of the fact that some Arabic scholars translate *asabiyya* not by 'cohesion' but with the word 'band' in the meaning of I Samuel 22, 2: 'Men in any kind of distress or in debt or with a grievance gathered round (David) . . . and he became their chief.' But whether 'cohesion' or 'band' is what *asabiyya* stands for, Ibn Khaldun looks back with nostalgia to the beginning of the impetus of every history which, if disappearing, leads to inevitable decline. So does Gibbon. Gibbon and Ibn Khaldun are aristocrats, men of a society in which medieval feudal elements are still alive. Their aristocratic attitude was also represented by a German romantic poet, who wrote under the name of Novalis and whose real name was Friedrich von Hardenberg (1772-1801). His poem *wenn alle untreu werden, so bleiben wir doch treu* (If all abandon faith, we still remain faithful) was included into the Songbook of the S.S. by order of Hitler. But more connections with the romantic poet and Nazism have to be considered. Where Ibn Khaldun speaks of *asabiyya* as the creative origin of history, Novalis has the word *voelkisch* (derived from *Volk*, nation). The three noblemen Ibn Khaldun, Gibbon and Novalis look backwards. The prophets, even the stern Amos, look forwards. Messianism is hope.

65

The German word *voelkisch* is untranslatable into any non-German language. This word alone makes the roots of Nazism understandable. Novalis uses the word *voelkisch* of the medieval feudal society, which unhappily — so it seemed to him — was dislocated by modern urban society. Those who look back to *asabiyya*, to a *voelkisch* period, can only be pessimistic about history with its inevitable cycle of the rise and fall of civilizations.

In Ibn Khaldun's theory of the fall of civilizations there looms the fear of what our modern theorists call the inevitability of the historic process. Ibn Khaldun sees eternity as timelessness. The sun of the desert burns down on the sand, in which nothing living can exist. This terrifying prospect drives man to permissiveness. Our terrifying prospect is 'the bomb'. 'Therefore let us be merry, as long as it is possible. The end is inevitable.' The Muslim's faith is faith in kismet. The Muslim in Ibn Khaldun regards the end of civilization as inevitable. He is either paralysed by this prospect or driven into a permissiveness which leads to a polygamous sex life. Jew and Christian affirm the holiness of monogamy. They retain in the family *asabiyya*, which in the midst of history gives power to civilization and makes it lasting. Jew and Christian accept the lesson which Jonah receives and which brings good tidings to civilization standing on guard against the barbarians. 'And should I not be sorry for the great city of Nineveh, with its hundred and twenty thousand who cannot tell their right hand from their left, and cattle without number?' (4, 11).

Ibn Khaldun is a Muslim, but must not be regarded as typical of Islam. Islam must be seen, in spite of Ibn Khaldun, as a monotheistic religion like Judaism and Christianity. But Mohammed's stern doctrine of the 'Day of Judgement' is typically Islamic. Amos' sermon about the 'Day of the Lord' leaves the door wide open for hope. Amos is not a prophet of despair. Ibn Khaldun is the archetype of a historian whom the contemplation of history has made a prophet of despair. Sartre, Camus, Toynbee, George Steiner are prophets of despair. The years of economic depression and unemployment, Hitler's victories, the holocaust, Vietnam were challenges which many could not

bear. They despaired. They had their philosophical mouthpiece in Martin Heidegger who says of man in history that 'he
runs forward towards death'. But there is God's command: 'go
to a country that I will show you' (Genesis 12, 1). Walking with
Abraham through history means walking forward in hope.

The Torah (and the Gospel) as Koran
Mohammed is called *al-Nabi al-Ummi*, 'the prophet whose
mission is for the "unlettered" '. The Koran is 'scripture for the
unscriptured'. (I prefer this translation, which is by Bishop
Kenneth Cragg, to that of Arberry, 'the common people'.)
'Unlettered', 'unscriptured' does not refer to people who cannot read and write. It refers to people whose faith is not based
on the Torah of the Jews and on the Gospel of the Christians.
These books of Jew and Christian were written by writers,
scholars and poets, the latter most hated by Mohammed, who
was strongly concerned that revelation should not be seen as a
poet's vision. The Koran is a book, but Islam teaches that it is
not a book, it is a miracle. The Koran is not from the world of
learning either, but from the world of 'Mount Hira and the
shadow of the wing of Gabriel'. The Koran is Koran through its
connection with the archangel Gabriel — this is the Islamic
doctrine, which in a Jewish formulation proclaims: the Torah is
from heaven (*Torah min hashamayim*).
    As the prophet of the *ummi*, of the 'unlettered', Mohammed
brought to these 'unlettered' people, to people who did not have
a holy book like the Jews and the Christians, a book. Men
'without the book and without wisdom' received a book. It was
not a literary event when the Koran became the possession of
the Arab people. It was the miracle of revelation. Jew and
Christian say that the ways of God are beyond understanding.
The Muslim will also say so. But, above all, he says of the Koran
itself that it is beyond human understanding.
    When my pious grandmother said 'One of my sons must
devote his life to the study of the Torah,' she did not know that
the Torah was a compendium to which scholars, prophets,
poets, indeed, writers of all kinds had contributed. To her, the

67

pious Jewess, the Torah belonged to the realm of miracle, as did the Koran to the Muslim. What she called Torah was a Jewish Koran. True, it was a book, but a book from heaven.

When Karl Barth, writing for a highly sophisticated circle of theologians, rejected Harnack's scientific historical analysis of the Old and New Testament Scriptures and spoke in a complicated dialectic of the 'Word of God' not to be identified with any written text, he did what Mohammed did. He excluded scholars, historians and philosophers — Mohammed would say poets — from those capable of a right approach to revelation. They cannot assist in the transmission of the 'Word of God'. The subtle dialectical theology of Karl Barth saw the Gospel as my pious grandmother saw the Torah: as a miracle. He saw the Gospel as a Christian Koran. What makes the Koran what it is is a quality which neither reason nor imagination can fathom. Medieval man, be he Jew or Christian, interpreted the Holy Scriptures as the Muslim interpreted the holiness of the Koran. Historical criticism put and end to this Islamic theology, which Jewish and Christian Orthodoxy have not yet repudiated even today. The sentence 'Moses died' in the Fifth Book of Moses cannot have been written by Moses himself. Who wrote it? God himself 'wrote' the sentence. In this way modern Jewish Orthodoxy, an offshoot of the nineteenth century, defends the doctrine that Moses is the only author of the Pentateuch. Modern Jewish Orthodoxy, walking still in the nineteenth and twentieth centuries in the footsteps of medieval man, makes the Five Books of Moses a Jewish Koran. Modern Jewish Orthodoxy refuses to agree that the Torah is a product of history. It refuses to be emancipated from the Middle Ages. The emancipation from the Middle Ages is an emancipation from Islam. Historical criticism of the Scriptures, rightly hailed by the progressive approach of Rabbi Abraham Geiger as bringing light into Jewish history, and even tolerated by the Vatican's official biblical studies, is rejected by Jewish Orthodoxy. The Bible of Jewish Orthodoxy, its Torah, is a Koran.

The emancipation from the Middle Ages becomes a political issue within the young State of Israel. Islam's social background is the medieval feudal society. The Israeli rabbis insist on upholding the status which they had in the Polish feudal past. The Eastern European medieval rabbi had no political power. He had to establish his superiority over the rank and file of his flock through an assumption of charismatic qualities. But now it is different. The State of Israel has acknowledged the Jewish law in its pre-Emancipation character. The modern Jew in Israel is trapped in a society in which he is chained to a law as if he were a medieval Muslim. Islamic law (from which even some modern Muslims are beginning to emancipate themselves) is, according to the *ulema,* the Muslim divines, a law which cannot be reformed. The Israeli Orthodox rabbi too points to a Jewish law, which is, in fact, the Torah transformed into a Koran. The *Kulturkampf* in Israel makes us return to the arguments of the theologians of Progressive Judaism. We thought the struggle for emancipation was a settled victory. The reactionary rabbis in the State of Israel (and elsewhere) force us to begin all over again. We must stop those who make our Torah a Koran. The *halachah,* the law sanctified as Torah, must again be derived from Micah 6, 8: 'God has told you what is good; and what is it that the Lord asks of you? Only to act justly, to love loyalty, to walk wisely before your God.' Here alone we face the law which is eternal law. Every other law added to the one which Micah proclaims is, as a product of history, changeable, capable of reform. The *halachah* of the Israeli rabbinate serves the vested interests of a clergy which, because it is a clergy, is most un-Jewish. The *halachah* which preserves mere folklore and a soulless ritualism must again be made to serve the only one eternal law: the moral law. This is the aim of the theological struggle of Progressive Judaism. This struggle is unavoidable. The *Kulturkampf* in Israel is unavoidable. Israel needs the teachings of Progressive Judaism and with their help the Torah will be restored to its holiness. With the help of the theology of Progressive Judaism the Torah in Israel will cease to be an Islamic Koran.

The word Talmud like the word Torah must also be approached by theological critical analysis. Zunz wrote: 'As long as the Talmud is not dethroned, nothing can be done.'*

*See Nahum N. Glatzer (ed.), *Leopold and Adelheid Zunz*, London 1958, p. xv.

When he wrote these words he was not yet the scion of Jewish learning. He was an adolescent complaining about the lack of a proper method of studying the Talmud. This antiquated method is no longer our concern. Historians, philosophers, grammarians, all sorts of modern scholars — Jewish and non-Jewish — have brought order into the thicket of the Talmud and have succeeded in separating the various texts from each other. The Talmud is no longer seen as an unsystematic encyclopaedia, in which the subject matter is recorded without the help of proper guidance. It is now easily accessible and we can study it in its separate parts: Jewish law, Jewish history, Jewish sermons *(haggadah)* and so on. The complaint of Zunz no longer bothers us.

Yet circumstances, which modern Jewish Orthodoxy is guilty of bringing about, again make it necessary to say: 'As long as the Talmud is not dethroned, nothing can be done.' The Talmud has become the 'good book'. It is so wherever modern Jewish Orthodoxy has its political influence, in Israel and in the diaspora. The Talmud as the 'good book' makes Jewish society similar to a Muslim society. The Muslim sees himself as a slave of God. 'Child of God' is a Jewish and Christian concept, not understandable to the Muslim. The Muslim unquestioningly renders obedience to a book, the Koran. Islam is a book religion. In all this — a book holy like God, obedience which must never be questioned — we are describing a medieval feudal society.

When modern Orthodoxy makes the Talmud a 'good book', a holy document, derived from outside history, freedom of thought has disappeared. The laws of the Talmud, elevated to holiness, must not be questioned. This means that a docile community is at the mercy of rabbis who reject any interpretation of a progressive nature. A *Kulturkampf* is necessary to prevent the Jewish community from becoming like a Muslim community with the religious leaders acting as defenders of a feudal society, a static society, in which clergy and politicians co-operate to prevent change. The Talmud must be 'dethroned'. It is not a question of how many laws recorded in the Talmud are petrified and even immoral. It is not a question

70

of how many represent wisdom and admirable moral sensitivity. The Talmud which does not allow freedom of thought, the Talmud as the 'good book', the Talmud which has become a fetish, must be dethroned.

The word Torah is imbued with transcendence, so much so that is can be seen as equal to the word revelation. The Talmud is an historical document, and we might be tempted to say that it has served for centuries as a Magna Charta of the Jewish people. But neither the Magna Charta nor the Talmud can be regarded as a sacrament. Futhermore, there is the term 'Jewish law'. Torah is translated as law, Talmud referred to as the book of laws of the Jewish people. The translation of Torah as 'law' is the translation promulgated by Paul. This translation must be rejected by Jews; it has been enforced on us from outside. Paul translates Torah with *nomos*, with state law. It is in this way that he saw the Torah. For two thousand years this Pauline translation has caused monumental misunderstandings. It is time that we Jews closed this chapter of Jewish history and ceased to call the Torah law. The Torah is all that has guided the Jewish people and will guide the Jewish people on its way to God.

71

V

The Jewish Family

Monotheism and Monogamy

THE age-old confrontation of home and history is today more
than ever with us. Elijah's fury against Ahab and Jezebel has its
reason in his view that the values which make the home of the
family a holy place get lost in history. But God, the one and only
God, is met in history and where the family lives that way of life
which is at all times a patriarchal one. The word 'patriarchal'
must not be misunderstood. A patriarchal family — even in this
our twentieth century — is when a husband and his wife and
children unite into a group in which law and love bind them
together. A family is not created by history. The family represents an eternal, unchanging order. History is continually
changing. History is the place of creative man, and creative
man, best represented by the artist, moves from one task to the
next. History never stands still. Families populate the realm of
history. But if today families do not remain what they were in
the days of the biblical patriarchs, if families are consumed to be
mere material for history, if families do not withstand the
pressure of the permissive society, history decays, civilizations
decline and die like plants without sun and water. Western man
lives in history. But when he becomes a man of the mass age,
when he becomes uprooted from the family, he has nothing to
contribute to civilization. Man in history can be a liberator or a
destroyer. When Hitler came to power, he said *'Jetzt wird
Geschichte gemacht'* (Now we shall make history). The work of
man who is nothing but a 'political animal', man outside the
family, is only destructive.

As long as men rooted in their families populate history, it
will be a place of happiness. Creative man is not a destroyer of
human happiness as long as he is rooted in his family. The

family is a monogamous unit or it is not a family. Judging by the biography of many an artist, monogamy is too much to ask from him. But with the insistence on monogamy we approach the very depth of religious life. Monogamy and monotheism belong to each other. Monotheism will stay with us as long as Jewish-Christian civilization lasts. Here we speak of Jewish-Christian civilization and exclude Islam. Islam does not accept monogamy. But it does not accept polygamy either. Islam allows monogamy to be reduced according to the social need of the primitive agricultural life in which those at the bottom of the feudal system manage the heavy work. More than one woman is needed for the work in which the Muslim uses his wives as a labour force. Jew and Christian are horrified at this slavery within marriage. But Islam discovered early the close connection between monotheism and monogamy: 'Must not the inner love of husband and wife be as securely undivided as their love of God? Pluralism in worship diversifies an allegiance that should be unique: so also do concurrent and consecutive marriages. A man's whole heart cannot be wholly in two places, either Godward or wifeward.' (Kenneth Cragg, *The Dome and the Rock,* S.P.C.K., London 1964)

Gifts donated to the Temple are, according to biblical law, consecrated, remain holy and are not to be exposed to profanation. Such consecration binds man and woman together in marriage, and their bond is an holy order. From out of a host of men and women two people are segregated from all other men and women and are consecrated to each other and dedicated to their sole companionship. Monogamy, like everything concerning the rules of the Temple worship, is not merely a social form of life, it is a holy order. Jewish-Christian monotheism, affirming the Oneness of God, demands a oneness which every married couple represents. Monogamy is like monotheism. Both exist through faithfulness to a unique oneness. Isaiah formulates the uniqueness of God with the words of God: '. . . nothing besides Me' (45, 6). An invocation of the unique oneness also takes place at the wedding ceremony. The unique oneness of God and the unique oneness of the relationship between one man and one woman are both affirmed in the

'Hear, O Israel, the Lord is One.' Monotheism and monogamy both have the same message: the appeal to a unique and holy oneness.

Monotheism and monogamy exist. But so do polytheism and polygamy. History is polytheistic. Nation, State, affluent social life and many other gods make it so. History is the field where creative man is fascinated not by one but by many goals, and the artist who is the archetype of creative man is anything but a puritan. But the day comes when creative man asks himself: 'How long shall I be what Cain is, "a vagrant and a wanderer on earth"?' (Genesis 4, 12). The crisis overwhelms the artist when he recognises that 'a thing of beauty' is not 'a joy for ever'. The same crisis is known to those who invest all they have in history. Franz Rosenzweig, the greatest *homo religiosus* modern Jewry has brought forth, movingly describes the crisis of creative man: 'many great artists have sooner or later taken leave of the falsehood of artistic life and cast their magic wand with Prospero into the sea in order to live out their lives humanly, as simple mortals, in some Stratford or other. For the thinker will one day place his thoughts before God's throne, and the doer his deeds, in order to be judged in their midst. But the artist knows that his works will not follow him, that he must leave them behind on that earth whence they sprang, like everything which does not belong to the whole human being' (*Star*, p. 190).

Rosenzweig is rooted in his Jewish faith and yet uses Christian semantics in the book of his youth, *The Star of Redemption*. In this he is the typical post-medieval Jew who sometimes speaks like a Christian. This is not a sign of wavering between Judaism and Christianity. He uses without hesitation the metaphor seed-tree, Christianity growing from Judaism, Christianity enclosed within Judaism. Thus the devout Jew Franz Rosenzweig speaks of the Cross. But he does not yet speak in the way of Christian semantics when he writes: 'Prometheus already hung suspended from the rock half a millenium before the cross was raised on Golgotha.' (*Star*, p. 376). This sentence could have been written by any scholar of comparative religion. It is not a confession of a Christian. But we descend into the profound depth of Christian faith when we read: 'Art indeed appears to replace the cross in the fullest measure' (ibid., p. 377). Creative man uprooted from home and family and being entirely busy as creator in history must necessarily end as man on the cross. History is Golgotha, a place of skulls (this is the literal translation of the word Golgotha). Every place in the world where history has been fought out is marked by a cross under which lie those who suffered, bled and died. These numerous crosses, alleges the Christian, are different from the one Cross, which is the Cross of Golgotha. According to the Christian only this Cross redeems history. Rosenzweig points with respectful, even warm understanding to this Christian doctrine. Needless to say, he does not make it his own.

History is always political. Christianity is able to bring redemption to history by transforming gentiles into Christian gentiles. Jews are not gentiles, because they are rooted not in history, but in the family. The Jew receives redemption as an individual, the Christian as a member of his national and political group. Yet redemption is there for Jew and Christian. God is the Redeemer of all who live. What made Rosenzweig a non-Zionist was his conviction that Jews becoming gentiles will find that Christianity and not Judaism is able to solve the problems in which a Jewish State involves them.

> Why are the nations in turmoil?
> Why do the people hatch their futile plots?
> The kings of the earth stand ready,
> and the rulers conspire together
> against the Lord and his anointed king.
> 'Let us break their fetters,' they cry,
> 'Let us throw off their chains!'
> The Lord who sits enthroned in heaven
> laughs them to scorn;
> then he rebukes them in anger,
> he threatens them in his wrath.
>
> (Psalm 2, 1-5)

But this condemnation of history by the Psalmist cannot be his last word. How often is he full of praise and gratitude for the islands of happiness in history. The Jew sees history moving towards its messianic goal. God is, and so is man, but the world is still becoming. 'The world is not yet finished. Laughter and weeping are still in it. The tears are not yet "wiped away from every countenance" ' (*Star*, p. 219). The Jewish divine service anticipates the future in the *kaddish*, a prayer glorifying God as King over all the earth. Home and history both, in a different way, have their messianic relevance.

This subtle theological discourse has a very practical background. Rosenzweig was not a Zionist. The controversy between assimilation and Zionism must not be seen — as it still is today — as a chapter of Jewish history in which the Zionist faced an ignoble opponent. Both the so-called assimilationist movement, the theology of any diaspora, and Zionism were messianic movements, the one making the home the place of a truly religious hope, the other looking to history for the fulfilment of its expectations. The Liberal said 'progress' and meant the Kingdom of God, the Zionist said 'national renaissance' and meant Zion, the residence of God in the midst of the world. Whether it was European gentile history by means of which the post-medieval Jew hoped to put an end to Jewish suffering through assimilation to western forms of life, or whether it was Jewish nationalism which was expected to offer this solution, in both cases trust in history and emancipation from a Jewish home made the Jew leave the Middle Ages. Boys reared in Jewish homes threw themselves into history and won the Six Days War.

The home is and remains the abode of the Jew. But a Jewish home cut off from history can become the essence of Jewish decadence. Before leaving Russia for France the young Marc Chagall painted a remarkable picture which he called 'Sabbath' (reproduced in Alan Bullock, *The Twentieth Century*). We see an Orthodox Jewish family on a Friday evening. Chagall paints the members of this family as if they were paralysed in an immovable stiffness. The clock on the wall is the only thing which is 'alive'; its hands move. The caption of Chagall's painting reads: 'The orthodox family sits inactive, as the slow minutes tick away.' Orthodoxy made the Jewish home a stagnant place. Non-essential things became essential: no lighting of a fire, no switching on of electric light, no driving and so on.

From this stagnation Liberalism and Zionism liberated the Jew. The life of the Jew — in fact, the life of man — needs the warmth of the home and the fresh air of history.

Love and Marriage
The Orthodox Jewish prayer book has a benediction (already mentioned in the Talmud, *Menahoth* 43b) which reads: 'Blessed art thou, O Lord our God, King of the universe, who hast not made me a woman.' This is the point where Islam later penetrated Judaism most fully. Not only according to the doctrines of Islam but in the conviction of every male Muslim, woman has no 'soul' in the Christian sense nor is she a 'person' in the western legal sense. With this view of women Islam asserts a concept of history without any intervention of those values which Jew and Christian connect with the home as the place where all the members of the family are equally souls, where they are all persons. Islam understands history as being far removed from the world of the home. Love reigns in the home. The Muslim knows of mercy, not of love. A sermon in a mosque announcing 'God is love' is impossible. What we call love, the Muslim would call sex. In the home peace reigns. The Muslim speaks of resignation, which is not peace. A Jewish emancipation from Islamic influences restores classical, prophetic Judaism. In the centuries of Islamic influence on Jewish life a Jewish woman lived a degraded life. The prayer of the male worshipper 'Blessed art thou, O Lord, who hast not made me a woman' was justified in many respects.

Home and history are two different worlds. The man who comes from a home and is shaped by it will act differently in history from the man who has never experienced the blessings of home life. History devours its hecatombs of sacrifices. Youth, above all, is sacrificed. Each generation goes like Isaac to the altar, where a voice says: 'Give me your son!' This story, the *Akedah,* the 'binding of Isaac', is told in two narratives, one in Genesis, the other in the Koran. In Genesis we meet a father who represents both law and love. In the Koran there is a father who stands for law, but for law without love. In the first case the home of man penetrates history, in the second history goes on in inevitable tragedy without the intervention of love. In Genesis Abraham hears a voice not recorded in the Koran: 'Do not raise your hand against the boy; do not touch him' (22, 12).

Mohammed tells the story about Isaac in Sura 37 without mentioning any intervention from outside history. Only a history far removed from the home which harbours love determines the fate of the Koranic Isaac. The story as Genesis tells it is known wherever the redemptive power of God is praised. The story in the Koranic form is shortened and records the bitter command: 'Give me your son!' Abraham obeys. This is all and this is enough. The rescue of Isaac is added like a postscript which does not really belong to the story.

We urgently need a poet to create a female counterpart to the Muslim Isaac: a girl not redeemed but sacrificed. (Or have we got this figure in Goethe's Gretchen?). Such girls are numerous when the permissive society corrupts a generation of men and women. When a society goes in the wrong direction, the main sufferers are the women. They pay the price for the mistakes and sins of the men. In the permissive society women are degraded as they are in the role which Islam has allotted to them. The recurring reference to Islam in this book may be regarded as strange, but in the age of secularisation not only Christian values, but Islamic values too, shape our civilization. Their original place in their respective historic establishment is overlooked. Bourgeois and Muslims have more in common than either of them think. Both hold law in high esteem. Theirs is a law, alas, without love. The women's liberation movement is not emancipation from medieval and modern Islamic civilization, but is a new involvement in it. The woman of 'women's lib' wants freedom not as a soul, not as a person, but as a gender. But happy marriages, indeed a happy way of life, demand that both law and love shape human existence. Love needs to be rehabilitated both from Pauline spirituality and from the Islamic identification of love with sex.

Goethe pondered all the years of his old age — he died when he was eighty-two — how to finish his *Faust* with a Gretchen in heavenly glory. He could not do it. In the end, he, the Protest-

78

ant, concluded his work with a conventional Roman Catholic heaven and with Gretchen as Madonna. Many critics have said that this last scene of *Faust* is not credible. The old man wanted to express atonement. Before God Gretchen will not be denied atonement. But on earth she is a broken reed. Goethe suffered deep pain about the harm he had inflicted on Gretchen. Let the Gretchens of our times not be like the Koranic boy Isaac — sacrificed without redemption. Let them be like Isaac of the Book of Genesis, walking in union with his father, with Abraham, and saved, saved through union with a mother. 'I would lead you to the room of the mother who bore me, bring you to her house to teach me how to love you' (Song of Songs 8, 2). To the girls exposed to the dangers of the permissive society the Song of Songs calls out: 'I adjure you, O daughters of Jerusalem, by the gazelles, and the hinds of the field, that ye awaken not, nor stir up love, until it please' (ibid., 2, 7). In the Song of Songs 8, 1 the bride says to the bridegroom: 'If only you were my own true brother'. Our Hebrew Bible does not give us abstract theories. The Song of Songs is not a philosophy of love. But it is the most profound book dealing with love. Love in our Song of Songs is a dialogue between a human I and that Thou who is God. Love is both human and also holy love, the same love in which man loves God and God loves man.

Of this holy and human love the girl in the above-quoted verse sighs and sobs and longs for something which is not love but, as it says in Rosenzweig's commentary to the Song of Songs, 'more than love'. What is more than love? Marriage is, and therefore the girl says: 'If only you were my own true brother.' She wants love, this revolution in her soul, and marriage, this uninterrupted warmth of the many climates which make summer appear as a season without end. We turn again to Franz Rosenzweig's exegesis of the Song of Songs, where he says: 'Marriage is not love. Marriage is infinitely more than love. Marriage is the external fulfilment in which love reaches out from its internal blissfulness in a stupor of unquenchable longing — O that you were my brother . . .' (*Star*, p. 204).

The Holy Seed

The steadily rising number of intermarriages begins to worry even the most tolerant defenders of Jewish universalism. The Jewish liturgy reminds the worshipper again and again that the election of the Jewish people cannot and must not be explained away by universalism which, to be sure, both prophets and rabbis preach as the content of Judaism. The rabbis, although excluding proselytisation, teach Jews to welcome proselytes with kindness. On the other hand the election of the Jewish people is upheld as valid in all history, past, present and future. 'He has chosen us from all nations.' No conversion can transform a gentile into a Jew, no anathema can exclude a Jew from his Jewishness. Jewishness has no door through which Jews can get away from their Jewish existence and none which could let gentiles enter into the intimacy of the common Jewish bond. A Jew is born a Jew. He is part of the Jewish people through his physical existence. And a Jew cannot stop being a Jew. During the holocaust many a Jew may, like Jeremiah and Job, have cursed the day that he was born a Jew. But there was no way for him to get out. Considered in this way — and it is in this way that it must be considered — intermarriage does not bestow on the non-Jewish partner the Jewish particularity. Our praise of the universalism of Jewish teaching is sincere, but our insistence on the particularity which the election of the Jewish people implies cannot be given up. The objection to intermarriage is not primitive clannishness, not tribalism left over from the past, not racialism. Particularism is as justifiable as universalism. As universalism is the hallmark of our service to mankind so is our Jewish particularism. God has chosen the Jewish people, has set it apart from all the nations and has done so for the benefit of mankind. Jews are withdrawn from mankind in order to serve it.

The praise of Judaism as a universalistic faith abounds in modern Jewry. The defender of Jewish particularism is a lonely figure in our modern world. On the Jewish side there is only Franz Rosenzweig who defends it as a theologian. On the side of the Christians I know only Kenneth Cragg, who as a Christian theologian has profound things to say in defence of Jewish particularism. Here is a Christian who is not scandalised by Jewish particularism, but sees it as the fertile ground from which his own Christian universalism grew.

The confrontation particular-universal is formulated by Franz Rosenzweig in the confrontation of 'spiritual' and 'a community of common blood'. 'We' — note the proud 'we' — 'have no need to hire the services of the spirit: the natural propagation of the body guarantees its eternity' (*Star*, p. 299). Ezekiel's 'In thy blood live!' (16, 6) demands loyalty to the election of the people. This election is not divine favouritism. It is the God-created way through which the particular can serve the universal, the Jewish people can serve mankind. The promise of God to Abraham '. . . So shall thy seed be' (Genesis 15, 5) is the promise to every father who is truly human in his hope that he will be the progenitor of descendants who will not quickly disappear but will last 'from generation to generation'. Intermarriage cannot but be a sad interruption or even an ending of this flow of blood, sanctified for perpetuity, for eternity.

The loyalty of Jewry to its common blood community is not racialism. Blood is not holy, what is holy is God's promise of eternity which the blood is destined to carry through the ages. Blood is the human vehicle. All men are human as creatures in whose veins flows blood, the same blood.

Any vocation is open to abuse. Yet community of birth, common ancestry, the awe in which we speak of the 'holy seed', the precious intimacy which cannot be decried as clannishness — all this served as a mighty constituent of Jewish loyalty. All this gets lost — or at least can get lost — when intermarriage takes place. That Jews throughout the centuries willingly listened to those who preached against 'marrying out' explains the miracle of the Jewish people, the miracle of its continuity. In the self-understanding of the Jewish people as 'the chosen people' the outcry 'our fathers' is not a reference to a genealogy but a confession of the abiding trust which preserved the Jewish people for its vocation throughout history. The proud 'we' — the Jewish cry 'but "we" are eternal' — is in the key of a passionate, humble and blissful psalm.

81

Of course every people is a chosen people. Nature, territory, climate, history create a unique identity in every nation. The gentiles become nations by claiming the possession of a unique identity. But the unique, mysterious identity in the ethnic existence of the Jewish people is not the work of nature, territory or climate. It is not enough to say, as Bishop Kenneth Cragg does, that Jewish election exists in the belief of those who believe themselves to be chosen. This statement is true but not sufficient; above all, it misses the crux of the matter. The Jew is chosen, whether or not he accepts or knows this fact. The election of the Jewish people is not a mere belief, a mere doctrine or — least of all — a mere idea. It exists in brute acutality. We can see the actuality of Jewish election at work, as we see the dark skin of a negro or the colour of a person's eyes. In order to make Jewish election visible like any matter which can be seen and touched, like any event which can be witnessed as occurring in history, we must keep in mind the situation of Jew, Christian and Muslim in their relationship to the State.

The Jewish people living under the conditions of the diaspora, living as a people of exiles, has an attitude to force, to political power which is different from that of Islam. Christianity is sometimes 'Jewish' in its attitude to the State, sometimes, especially as a Constantinian Church, its attitude to the State is identical with Islam. Islam is a political religion. The Caliphate is a State religiously conceived and revered. Islam finds it natural and even stipulates that the prophet becomes ruler. This contradicts everything which we know of the biblical prophet. Islam understands piety as obedience, it looks for piety not in conviction but in a legal attitude. Victory on the battlefield is the victory of God. Success in political affairs is proof of God's intervention. God is identified with success. The community of the faithful is 'the party of God' (Sura 5, 56). The State is called to assist religion, violence is necessary. The Muslim sees his political enemy as an enemy of God. The Muslim is an iconoclast. But all this having been said, it must also be remembered that Islam is a monotheistic faith and one which can penetrate into Judaism and into Christianity. Jew and Christian have to be aware of

82

this ever-possible penetration.

The Jewish people, dispersed among the nations, has no access to power. To exist in history without power — is this possible? From the year 70 C.E. to 1948 the Jewish people could not shape its fate by using power. The establishment of the State of Israel has changed this predicament. Geography, however, makes any State established on Israel's soil a buffer state dependent on super-powers. It rules out a reliance on power alone. There is now a difference between diaspora Jewry and the Israeli. The one has not, the other has, access to force. But this difference is not such as to allow Israel the reckless use of power. The refusal to employ force to destroy evil can be seen after Auschwitz as belonging to the realm of eschatology, which must not guide man destined to live in history. The blessing and the curse of existing without power is at the root of the election of the Jewish people. The Jewish people calls itself 'the merciful people, children of merciful people'. This is not sermonic hyperbole. It means what it says. A sociologist as a scientist and as a seculariser could use this phrase as a correct scientific description of the Jewish people. The social and political circumstances shaping the Jewish people as the people of the diaspora made it a 'merciful people'. Christians hail mercy as a Christian virtue, Muslims call mercy the foremost attribute of God — *Allah rahman* — but mercy as Christian and Islamic dogma is one thing and mercy as a national, as the Jewish ethnic characteristic, another. Mercy — *rahmanut* — is the characteristic feature of the 'chosen people', of the Jewish people. The Jew, always reacting with *rahmanut,* diplays in this reaction his psychological nature.

This characteristic feature of the Jewish people is threatened when Judaism becomes a political religion. The urgent aim is to be a devoted Israeli patriot and to remain a Jew. The Jew of this post-holocaust age will be able to be a loyal Jew in Israel and everywhere in the diaspora and yet refuse to have the Torah politicised. Every national war tends to be a holy war, a *jihad* as the Muslim calls it. We shall have to avoid this temptation. A 'promised land' is not a national territory but the land which 'God will show' us, in Israel *and* in the diaspora. 'Service',

83

avodah, does not merely concern citizenship. Service is for the Jew the worship of God.

The Christian Church is a spiritual institution. Islam as a post-Christian religion regards such an institution as not viable in history and supplements it with its concept of a religious State. Neither Church nor Caliphate should be a blueprint for a Jewish State. The Jewish people as a people living under the conditions of a diaspora is called by the biblical prophet a 'remnant'. The Prophet says of the 'remnant' that he will 'remain'; man without power will not be devoured by those who have power. If this is true — and the history of the Jewish people shows it to be true — it is a miracle manifest as truth. This miracle surrounding the Jewish people as the 'remnant' makes it the 'chosen people'. In his *Star of Redemption* Franz Rosenzweig gives us a portrait of the remnant:

> '. . . Judaism, and it alone in all the world, maintains itself by subtraction, by contraction, by the formation of ever new remnants. This happens quite extensively in the face of the constant external secession. But it is equally true also within Judaism itself. It constantly divests itself of un-Jewish elements in order to produce out of itself ever new remnants of archetypal Jewish elements. Outwardly it constantly assimilates only to be able again and again to set itself apart on the inside. In Judaism there is no group, no tendency, nay barely an individual who does not regard his manner of sacrificing incidentals in order to hold on to the remnant as the only true way, and himself therefore as the true "remnant of Israel". And so he is. In Judaism, man is always somehow a remnant. *He is always somehow a survivor* (my italics), an inner something, whose exterior was seized by the current of the world and carried off while he himself, what is left of him, remains standing on the shore.'

(pp. 404–405)

Rosenzweig was not inclined to write a pamphlet against intermarriage. Nor did he in his time see any need for it. He was and

84

remained a Germanophile and lived in his small closed society of a Jewish-Christian circle which listened to his interpretation of Judaism. Standing out in this interpretation is the earlier-quoted statement: '. . . we (Jews) need not hire the services of the spirit: the natural propagation of the body guarantees (our) eternity.' Actually this was not written against intermarriage of which it implies a condemnation. It was written to exclude a spiritual, i.e. a Christian, interpretation of Judaism. The 'remnant' exists in history, real and visible. He walks on the roads of the world, and people who meet him find him different from others who pass by and call him Jew.

The Jewish people is the 'chosen people'. This privilege, which we hold in trust for the benefit of mankind is — as was pointed out earlier — threatened by two facts: by the rising number of intermarriages and by the politicisation of the Torah. Will there now be two forms of Jewish existence, one for the diaspora Jew and one for the Jewish citizen of the State of Israel? Only the former will be the Jew with his unique characteristic of being chosen. Europe has lost its aristocracy in the various wars and revolutions. Shall we — in this political ice age — lose our Jewishness of being 'merciful children of merciful fathers'? We feel we shall overcome the great crisis.

Those who 'join the House of Israel' are called 'proselytes of righteousness'. They may very well enrich the Jewish people. We should not call them 'converts' to Judaism. Conversion is a Christian not a Jewish experience. Race is not an obstacle to joining the House of Israel. There is the promise of the biblical prophet that 'a remnant will remain'. The Jewish people with its proud 'We' will continue to sing: 'We are Thy people, and Thou art our God.'

We live in a time when Judaism, Christianity and Islam penetrate each other doctrinally. But neither Jew nor Christian nor Muslim wants this doctrinal penetration to lead to a loss of the identity of the Jewish, Christian or Muslim religion. There is a difference between believing and belonging. What the *beth din* (the rabbinical Court) has to find out concerns the second more than the first. When the proselyte says 'we Jews', he should be accepted into the Jewish fold, even if his doctrinal knowledge of Judaism is not yet satisfactory. Are Jews born as Jews always more erudite in this respect?

Here we can learn from Islam. The Muslim stresses belonging, the Christian believing. Sura 49, which has the title *The Private Apartments*, refers in verse 14 to some Beduin people who came to Mohammed after he had become the ruler in Medina. These Arabs from the desert, who were not yet familiar with the details of the new faith of Islam, avowed their allegiance to it. Mohammed was fully aware that their determination to belong to Islam could not be a belief in Islam. The difference between believing and belonging must not be ignored. It was true kindness on the part of Mohammed that he was satisfied with the wish of these newcomers to belong to Islam without being capable of satisfactorily believing in Islam. Only the future can show whether their belonging to Islam will make them true believers. When a father gives his daughter away at the wedding, it is in God's hand whether the marriage will turn out to be successful. Rabbis, accepting a proselyte, cannot, even after their scrutinising interrogation, know if the newcomer will adapt himself to the Jewish community, and they will have to leave it to God who, if He wills it, will enrich the House of Israel by the entry of a new member.

VI

Summary

Part One

JUDAISM is a movement which aims at working for justice, loving mercy and walking humbly with God. In biblical semantics this movement is 'Exodus from Egypt and progress towards the Holy Land'.

A Christian talking about Christianity would begin his introduction by talking about an unchangeable doctrine, a Muslim about an unchangeable law. In the movement in which the Jew is involved neither doctrine nor law constitutes its Jewish character. Judaism is authentic when constituted by prophecy. Christianity is constituted by revelation. We find the historical and psychological data which are the elements of prophecy foremost in the Old Testament. The data which amount to revelation are in the New Testament. But everybody can at some time himself experience these phenomena without the help of historical precedents. Every Jew can experience Isaiah's vision of God as King of the universe. Every Christian can like Paul walk the Damascus road.

Prophet means speaker. He speaks, and his word is the word of God. The word of God is the word spoken by man. Listen to the word spoken by man to his neighbour. You may hear the word of God. Hear, O Israel. Listen to the dialogue between man and man. Judaism is prophetic; it is not in need of the two Christian experiences of revelation and faith (*pistis*).

The word revelation came into the vocabulary of mankind through a Hellenist who translated the Bible into Aramaic. He came to the passage 'God came down . . .' (Exodus 19, 20). As a man of Greek enlightenment he disliked the passage showing God in anthropomorphic form and translated the words 'God came down' as 'God revealed himself'. The Hebrew text 'God came down' says of God: 'He is in our midst and walks at our side.'

The terms revelation and faith are to be seen as relevant only to Christianity and never to Judaism or Islam. When Maimonides says 'I believe' he is a prisoner of the Arabic language. With his 'I believe' he says: 'I am loyal'. The word belief in the Hebrew Bible *(emunah)* means firmness. The torturing questions 'Do I believe?', 'Do I not believe?' cannot affect the Jew. Nor does it affect the Muslim. The Koranic term 'Abraham, the *hanif*' shows Abraham meeting God without being seen as tied to a denomination, to a 'religion'. What Bonhoeffer, a Christian martyr of our time, called 'religionless Christianity', and what Rosenzweig also formulated in this way sixteen years before Bonhoeffer, is what is meant by the concept of Abraham, the *hanif*. Abraham the *hanif* meets God without being a Jew or a Christian. Abraham the *hanif* — this Islamic term describes what a Jew is. You could not have a better description. In Prophetic Judaism the Jew meets God without the help of the concepts of revelation or law. 'Have your five senses open to the world, and God will be recognized as part of this world', Rosenzweig wrote to his mother (see *Trialogue*, p. 80). This is the religious realism of Franz Rosenzweig. It is characteristic of Judaism, justifiably called prophetic Judaism.

One feature of prophetic Judaism is its negative valuation of piety, of being *froom* (which is the medieval word for pious). Jews or Christians or Muslims can become (in the words of the Koran) 'pious idol worshippers'. Beware of the trap into which the pious can fall when they are only *froom* and devoid of any prophetic element in their religion. Prophetic Judaism is protected against falling entirely into the trap of mere piety. We need both prophet and priest as our guides. But the prophet must be more listened to when the hour comes to establish true Judaism.

Revelation and faith constitute Christian life. But any man can experience revelation and faith as psychological phenomena. He does so in the tempestuous upheaval on the Damascus road or in the pastoral peace emanating from the carol 'Silent Night'. A Jew can be moved by this carol but will not accept the message that on a certain date in history, in the year one, and in a certain place, in Bethlehem, history was not history but opened itself to the entry of the miracle. Jew and Muslim speak of God's presence, not limited to his appearance in one place and at one time.

A difference of a decisive nature exists between emancipated Judaism and Orthodox Judaism. Emancipation is emancipation from Islam, which dominated the medieval world. Orthodox, non-emancipated Jewry displays a Judaism which is often entirely Islamic in appearance. The main issue is the acceptance or rejection of biblical and post-biblical criticism. Islam and Jewish Orthodoxy accept the concept of an eternal law within history. *Sunna* on the side of Islam, the Orthodox *halachah* on the Jewish side, guard the immutability of this eternal law. You can run away from it but you cannot change it, say both the imam and the Orthodox rabbi. The concept of the oral law accepted by the Progressive rabbi makes change and progress possible. It is not true that, as the Orthodox rabbi and the imam say, a small brick taken away will make the whole building collapse. The Progressive rabbi, or simply the Jew, believes in the possibility of Reform. A westernised Judaism contradicts Orthodox Judaism and does so with success.

Contemporary Judaism therefore consists of two types of Jew, the one opting for the west, for progress and reason, and the other opting for the east. An Orthodox rabbi in Israel is an Islamised Jew. But the Jew who opts for the west and is successful in this endeavour is under the influence of Philo's concept of culture. Jewish culture originates, as I shall explain in a moment, in Christian culture and presupposes Jewish life in a western diaspora. We cannot reject — as does the Zionist — Jewish life under the conditions of the diaspora and at the same time crave for a Jewish culture. Jewish culture is the gift of the diaspora.

There is no biblical Hebrew word for culture. The word *tarbut*, which stands for culture, is a translation of the German word *Kultur*. It is helpful to turn to the word *avodah* which means two things: worship and work. Philo created a third meaning with the word *logos*.

89

Philo is a Jew confessing 'Hear, O Israel, the Lord our God is One.' Yet Philo is a Greek Jew fascinated by the glory of Greek culture, of Greek philosophy and of Greek art. Is he not bound to reject the glories of a culture which seem to contradict in their god-like beauty and power the oneness of God? Philo found a way out. He accepted the world of Greek civilization and called it the world of the *logos*. He became a disciple of Plato. The problem of the *logos*, which is not God but is raised in aesthetic admiration to lofty heights, even to holiness, is a problem which besets western Christianity with a dialectic which does not worry Jew or Muslim. With his 'Allah is Allah' the Muslim brushes away all the subtleties of western theology. But one thing is clear: western civilization glorified and emulated is Christianity, albeit 'Christianity Anonymous' (a term created by the Dutch theologian Arend T. van Leeuwen). Western culture is Christianity Anonymous. The modern Jew has to make a daily decision: should he turn to the east or the west? He will indubitably opt for the west, that is for Christianity, even if it is 'Christianity Anonymous'. He cannot in truth opt for the east, for Islam. Islam offers justice but it does not offer freedom. For Islam itself the same issue exists: a westernised Islam is not Islam.

What we called Judaism before the year 70 is not the same Judaism after this year. What we called Judaism before the European emancipation is not the same Judaism after this emancipation, which was the gift of the French Revolution. What we called Judaism before the holocaust of our time is not the same Judaism after this holocaust experienced by our generation. The historian must watch this variety changing from epoch to epoch. But the theologian, unlike the historian, must find Judaism in its unchangeable form, Judaism valid in all epochs and in all generations. The year 70, the year of the destruction of Jerusalem, shows Rome as a victorious world power opposing what the Jews stand for. The pagan Roman on the one side and the Jew on the other contradict each other with unalterable finality. What does a Jew stand for? Who is a Jew?

The answer given by the Israeli government was intended for the issue of the national identity card. It said: 'Anyone (is a Jew) who chooses in good faith to call himself a Jew and who does not profess any other religion.' Judged by common sense this is a satisfactory answer. But the Orthodox Israeli rabbinate protested. They went to war against all liberal formulations of the answer to the question: Who is a Jew? They wanted power. The *Kulturkampf* in Israel is on. A religious Judaism wielding secular power steps back to the situation which existed before the cataclysmic year 70 and its God-willed end of Jewish theocracy. The Orthodox rabbis in Israel demand the re-establishment of a theocracy by preaching religious nationalism. This is a reactionary step which western man, any liberal-minded man, must find abhorrent. If these Orthodox rabbis are successful, a great part of the Israeli citizenry is denied personal freedom.

Rome stands for military virtues, for fortitude in battle, for glory achieved on the battlefield, all noble virtues, but not Jewish virtues, even if the Jews have proved themselves as heroic fighters. Jewish virtues are kindness, charity, justice, humility. These virtues are summed up in the saying: 'Jews are merciful ones, children of merciful parents'. The State can reach for the nobility of military virtues, but the State must subdue mercy in the decisive hour of battle. Military man sheds blood mercilessly. Who is a Jew? A man shaped by mercy, his own and that of his forefathers. Mercy, characterising a man like a racial feature, makes the Jew. The Jew has a racial disposition for mercy, created by two thousand years of wandering. Jews are what the Muslim calls *dhimmis*, neither conquerors nor conquered. In this way they live outside the State. After 70, Jews lived a life outside the State, they were not soldiers but enhanced, as merchants and as professionals, the welfare of the nations in whose midst they lived. *Dhimmis* cannot be aggressive but can only exist as merciful people, children of merciful forebears. The genius of Islam discovered the answer to the question 'Who is a Jew?' It is man with mercy as a racial characteristic.

The Jew carries history in his blood, a history of two thousand years. Will this history, preserved by the Jew, get lost or will it be preserved? In any case it is still miraculously here in

91

this age of the holocaust. To call the Jew 'merciful man, offspring of merciful forefathers' is not to express an abstract doctrine; it is a reality, as friend and foe must acknowledge.

Whereas mercy is a reality expressing itself in action, vicarious suffering, just as noble, good and holy as any deed of mercy, is a doctrine. Every cross in the land heralds this doctrine. Its message is: somebody dies that you can live. The Muslim rejects this doctrine (Sura 4, 157). It is immoral, teaches the Koran, that an innocent man should die on the cross as a ransom. Jews agree with this Islamic teaching. But should they? Six million Jews died in the holocaust, many more millions of gentiles perished during World War II. Surely, the message of vicarious suffering warms our hearts, whereas the Islamic theology of the Cross gives us no hope. (The Islamic exegesis of the Cross, often readily accepted by Jews, must be seen as a welcome demythologisation of the Gospel story. The Gospel story, demythologised, belongs to monotheism.) Jew, Christian and Muslim must turn to the texts of Isaiah II and must in this way be united not merely as three differing schools of thought. In this study Jew, Christian and Muslim can become united like three brothers.

The most helpful contribution to this study is in my opinion given by the Christian theologian Kenneth Cragg, who writes: 'If some in the early Church needed to bring their Christ-devotion more carefully "into God", are there not some in the contemporary Church who need to reach out more readily from their Christology "into God"?' (*Alive to God: Muslim and Christian Prayer,* Oxford University Press, 1970, p. 24).

Cragg visualises a new type of Christian who no longer regards 'Christ-devotion' as the only way leading to God. That this new type of Christian is acknowledged in the Church of today is an event of cataclysmic importance. After two thousand years of Christian faith a new approach to Christ rises in Christendom. Obviously a Christian faith without Christ is impossible. But if contemporary Christian faith regards Jews and Muslims as able 'to reach out into God', a pagan element still lingering in the Christian Church is destroyed. Progress has happened. A new era has begun, because Jews, Christians and

92

Muslims acknowledge each other not merely on grounds of tolerance but with understanding of each other's religious message. Jews, Christians and Muslims have to vindicate the cataclysmic progress which monotheistic faith has achieved, or be taken as 'pious idol worshippers'. Jews praying in devotion at the Western Wall are 'pious idol worshippers'.

The question 'Who is a Jew?' burdens the individual Jew and challenges him. Can the individual Jew answer a question which requires a consideration of the whole of Jewish history? The answer forces the individual Jew to represent the whole Jewish people. No Jew can run away from his fate, from the conditions of his Jewish existence. The Jew is chosen. He may bless the Lord who has chosen him. He may curse his election, which does not let him go. The Jew is anchored in his Jewish fate. Anyone who asks the question 'Who is a Jew?' must be prepared to see an ordinary man, a man like any other man, but involved and implicated in the holy state of being elected by God.

The Christian is in a different situation. Ask a Christian 'Who is a Christian?' and, guided by his theologians, he must say: Nobody is a Christian except Christ. The Christian is a Christian through the help of what the Christian calls spirit. Who is a Christian? The answer is: man transported through faith to a spiritual realm, to the spiritual realm of the Church. The Jew is a Jew through being rooted in life, not spiritualised but sanctified. The difference between spiritual and holy leads to an understanding of the difference between Christian and Jew.

In the last 150 years western Jews, rabbis and historians, have shown a lively interest in a historical Jesus. They wrote about Jesus, depicting him as a reformer, as a socialist, as a Jewish patriot and nationalist, etc. To all this Albert Schweitzer put an end long ago. In his book *The Quest for the Historical Jesus* he told us that everyone who writes about Christ writes about himself. The historian paints his self-portrait.

Who is a Christian? He is a person who, with the help of the category of the spiritual, transforms his worship of God into the worship of that Christ with whom he has become familiar through the Gospels and through the history connected with the Gospels. Such a person prays to God and sees Christ standing before him. Such a person prays to God, and behold: God has a human face.

Who is a Muslim? It is incumbent on the scholars of comparative religion to discover the third possibility of monotheistic behaviour. A person is a Muslim insofar as he is a *mumin*, a loyal adherent of the religion into which he was born and in which he practises what he has learnt in his childhood and youth. Men are either loyal or — as Islam puts it — 'infidels'. Islam does not change a man's nature when he becomes a Muslim. It wants no progress. Mohammed was the last prophet, Islam teaches. Islam means resignation. Resignation does not mean peace, but is courageous and noble submission to the will of God. Islam wants uninterrupted tradition, it insists on the unchangeable *sunna*. Islam is conservative with regard to religion, whereas the Christian enters history with revolutionary zeal. The Christian is a crusader. The Jew remains involved in God's plan for mankind. The Jew is chosen: we can say nothing less when we answer the question 'Who is a Jew?'

Islam reduces *emunah*, the Jewish concept of prophetic faith, meaning firmness, to *iman*, meaning loyalty (*Shorter Encyclopaedia of Islam*, p. 167). The same reduction is applied by the Muslim to the Christian concept of faith acquired on the Damascus road. No Damascus road is needed when one becomes a Muslim. Who is a Muslim? The Muslim is a 'carrier' (in Karl Becker's phrase) of Judaism and Christianity. He also demythologises important parts of the New Testament and yet lets the Christian message remain a monotheistic message.

The language which the Ashkenazi Jews spoke in the Middle Ages was Yiddish. The Yiddish word *mensch* is still used today. In German the word *Mensch* means *homo sapiens*. But as a Yiddish word it means 'the whole man', man created in the image of God. 'Be a *mensch*,' addressed to man, means: be truly a man, be human! More than this God does not want from us. The Jew reminds all people that God has his habitat in this world in which we live and in which we are not deserted when we die.

94

Part Two

The three monotheistic religions, Judaism, Christianity and Islam, are different from and at the same time in some way identical with each other. What makes them different is their different historical situation. The State is spiritualised through Christianity and becomes a Church. The family is sanctified in Judaism and becomes a priestly order. Even the wild tribes of the desert become obedient to laws, understood as religious laws by the Muslim. In each of the three cases the one monotheistic message surges forth.

The challenging situation which Judaism answers is the situation of separate existence. Judaism is established, as we said before, with the application of the distinction between holy and profane. Holiness comes into existence through separation from the profane. To live under the conditions of the diaspora is to live with the help of separation. Every Jewish Liberal is annoyed by the dietary laws, but he will refrain from abolishing them. Jewish life in the diaspora is without the political cohesion of the nation state. As long as the dietary laws are not demythologised in a way which upholds the element of separation, Jews feel that they must keep them. It is as simple as that, and a Pauline interpretation of the Jewish law need bother no one. In obedience to Jewish law Jews obey the prophet and not the politician who has donned the garb of the priest.

The prophet is separated from the multitude. The Jewish people lives through separation from the other nations in a prophetic situation. Holy life is life in separation. It is the fate of the Jewish people to acquire holiness by sustaining and enduring the social existence of a diaspora people. Jewish history records Jewish existence as a western (Hellenistic) and as an eastern (Babylonian) diaspora. In both cases separation and also cooperation show life under the conditions of the diaspora as more human and more creative than is possible in any politically homogeneous group. Obviously an open society is human, a closed society lacks essential elements of truly human life. Yet no State, no Church, no Caliphate is an open society to such a degree as 'the people dwelling alone'.

The three monotheistic religions penetrate each other. In the case of 'Jewish' culture it has to be realised how much Christianity has penetrated Judaism. Jewish culture is, speaking not at all paradoxically, Christian culture. Culture presupposes the spiritual level and atmosphere which Christianity creates. The Christian dichotomy spiritual-secular is the force which adds a third dimension to the word *avodah*, namely culture. Culture is the Church in which creative man is the priest. As western culture is 'Christianity Anonymous' (Arend T. van Leeuwen), Jewish culture too is a world into which Christianity has opened a door through which Jews could enter and cooperate with the gentiles. Jewish culture is Christian culture Anonymous. In the splendid world of western culture the Jew is in fact in union with the Christian. The Jew has not been baptised. Baptism is not necessary where Jew and Christian are both creative in the field of culture. The help and assistance of the Jew can become highly important in this field. The contribution of the German Jews to western civilization is critically called mere synthesis by antisemites. But the synthesis can be as original and as important as the creative beginning itself.

Jewish culture is the gift of the diaspora in which the Jew receives from the creative Christian the possibility of becoming creative himself. In Jewish culture the Jew, who always sees himself as man the creature of God, becomes creative man. The Islamic rejection of human creativity — no art in the mosque (apart from the arabesque) is only one example — is made good in the tolerant admission of Jewish and Christian creative minds within Islamic culture.

The term Jewish culture, understood properly, must remind us of the mutual penetration of Judaism and Christianity and of the great harvest this mutual influence of the monotheistic religions has provided and will provide in the future. Jewish and non-Jewish historians speak of the golden age of the Jewish-Arabic culture. They have good reason to do so. But here too an anonymous participant, and not so anonymous at that, must not be overlooked: Islam. Judah ha-Levi, Maimonides and numerous others represent highlights in Jewish philosophy and poetry and also belong to the realm of Islamic civilization. But Jewish culture both in the west and in the east is not merely the imitation of the culture of its surroundings.

As a Christianity Anonymous exists, there exists also an Islam Anonymous. Marxism is Islam Anonymous. Marxism as a Messianic faith is the movement which German professors of philosophy, Hegel for instance, elaborated and called philosophy of idealism. God became an absolute idea. 'Progress', 'mankind', *Humanität* became substitutes for God. In defence of Islam as a true monotheistic religion we turn again to the term of the Islamist Karl Becker: 'Islam, a carrier of religion'. Islam is the carrier of monotheism. It could not be the carrier of say, Hinduism. Judaism can be established in Islamic surroundings, as it can be established in Christian surroundings. But it cannot be established in a culture shaped by Buddha.

The suggestion of Marxism as a fourth form of messianism, equal to the other three forms of messianism, Judaism, Christianity and Islam, has to be rejected, although it has been proposed by authorities like Leo Baeck and Hermann Levin Goldschmidt, the 'Frankfurter Kreis' (Adorno and Horkheimer), Herbert Marcuse and the Frenchman Roger Garaudy, who was expelled from the Communist party because of his attempt at reconciling Marxism with Christianity. Finally Franz Rosenzweig offers a valuable analysis of Islam, but unfortunately acknowledges only Christianity and Judaism as monotheism. That he does not regard Islam as a monotheistic religion has its reason in his Hegelian system of comparative religion. But any such system which does not include Islam as montheism is faulty.

Where nowadays scholars of comparative religion are tempted to see Islam even as superior to the other two monotheistic religions is in the field of worship. The Muslim at prayer has no assistance through art like the Christian. Prayer constitutes Islamic culture. The day is divided into sections, each with its allotted prayer of the *salat* (ritual prayer). Wild tribes rushing forward from the desert are taught the peace, the humility and the nobility which are the gift of prayer. This peace stops uncivilised people from being barbarians. Piety is to be found everywhere in the place of monotheistic civilization, but in

Islam piety constitutes a culture. It is not creative man, but man the creature of God, who shapes the way of life of the Muslim. This piety is not saintliness, it aligns itself to political tasks.

To acknowledge Islam, even to praise it, need not make us speak of a 'post-Christian era' which has caught up with us. Our age is not a post-Christian era, but follows the close of the Middle Ages. The Middle Ages were, as Rosenzweig calls them, the 'Pauline centuries'. They have ended. The English-speaking world will come to be shaped not by Pauline, but by Petrine Christianity. We should distinguish between Pauline, Petrine and Johannine Christianity. Together with Islam and Judaism they will be recognised as the religions of the new, monotheistic era.

The end of the Pauline centuries will at last bring to an end the fear of the Orthodox rabbi and the Imam, that even a slight reform of the law will shatter the whole edifice of the traditional law. The end of the Pauline centuries, or of the Middle Ages, implies an end of a slave-like obedience to a law to be emancipated from which means salvation. The way is free for a reform of Judaism. The way is free for a truly Jewish morality, which is sincere, sometimes strict, and avoids permissiveness. This attitude will not lead to obedience to a petrified ritualism. The way is also free for a Christianity which the lonely, mis-understood thinker Friedrich Nietzsche called a 'gay science'. We are freed from a law which oppresses man like a hard taskmaster. Post-medieval Judaism and post-medieval Christ-ianity make the way free also for Islam. God's salvation is always man's happy portion; it is not rendered to man at an historical date. There is no chronology of salvation. What is eternal has no history. The end of the Pauline centuries is the end of Paul's concept of law, driving us, sourly agreeing, to a moral life. To live according to the moral law is to live the life of salvation.

The Jewish people has survived for two thousand years since the destruction of Jerusalem by the Romans. It survived as an urban community. Can such a defenceless social unit survive in times like ours? This question needs to be asked and we cannot be sure about the answer. What we can say is this: If the Jewish community has no prospect of existing — as the Jewish people — in the western world, the western world has no prospect of survival either, nor has Christianity or Islam.

INDEX

105